D1080621

teach®
yourself

life at 50 – for men

This
Ad
da
b

**KENSINGTON & CHELSEA
LIBRARIES SERVICE**

Askews	
305.2441 ASH	
	PO-3967/2006

teach® yourself

life at 50 – for men
robert ashton

For over 60 years, more than 50 million people have learnt over 750 subjects the **teach yourself** way, with impressive results.

be where you want to be
with **teach yourself**

For UK order enquiries: please contact Bookpoint Ltd, 130 Milton Park, Abingdon, Oxon, OX14 4SB. Telephone: +44 (0) 1235 827720. Fax: +44 (0) 1235 400454. Lines are open 09.00–17.00, Monday to Saturday, with a 24-hour message answering service. Details about our titles and how to order are available at www.teachyourself.co.uk

For USA order enquiries: please contact McGraw-Hill Customer Services, PO Box 545, Blacklick, OH 43004-0545, USA. Telephone: 1-800-722-4726. Fax: 1-614-755-5645.

For Canada order enquiries: please contact McGraw-Hill Ryerson Ltd, 300 Water St, Whitby, Ontario, L1N 9B6, Canada. Telephone: 905 430 5000. Fax: 905 430 5020.

Long renowned as the authoritative source for self-guided learning – with more than 50 million copies sold worldwide – the **teach yourself** series includes over 500 titles in the fields of languages, crafts, hobbies, business, computing and education.

British Library Cataloguing in Publication Data: a catalogue record for this title is available from the British Library.

Library of Congress Catalog Card Number: on file.

First published in UK 2006 by Hodder Education, 338 Euston Road, London, NW1 3BH.

First published in US 2006 by The McGraw-Hill Companies, Inc.

The **teach yourself** name is a registered trade mark of Hodder Headline.

Copyright © 2006 Robert Ashton

In UK: All rights reserved. Apart from any permitted use under UK copyright law, no part of this publication may be reproduced or transmitted in any form or by any means, electronic or mechanical, including photocopy, recording, or any information, storage and retrieval system, without permission in writing from the publisher or under licence from the Copyright Licensing Agency Limited. Further details of such licences (for reprographic reproduction) may be obtained from the Copyright Licensing Agency Limited, of Saffron House, 6–10 Kirby Street, London, EC1N 8TS.

In US: All rights reserved. Except as permitted under the United States Copyright Act of 1976, no part of this publication may be reproduced or distributed in any form or by any means, or stored in a database or retrieval system, without the prior written permission of the publisher.

Typeset by Transet Limited, Coventry, England.
Printed in Great Britain for Hodder Education, a division of Hodder Headline, 338 Euston Road, London, NW1 3BH, by Cox & Wyman Ltd, Reading, Berkshire.

The publisher has used its best endeavours to ensure that the URLs for external websites referred to in this book are correct and active at the time of going to press. However, the publisher and the author have no responsibility for the websites and can make no guarantee that a site will remain live or that the content will remain relevant, decent or appropriate.

Hodder Headline's policy is to use papers that are natural, renewable and recyclable products and made from wood grown in sustainable forests. The logging and manufacturing processes are expected to conform to the environmental regulations of the country of origin.

Impression number   10 9 8 7 6 5 4 3 2 1
Year   2010 2009 2008 2007

contents

acknowledgements

To write a book that inspires men to make their 50s special, I needed to make reaching 50 special for myself. As this book will show you, that cannot be achieved alone and I need to acknowledge the enthusiastic support of everyone who worked with me as that magic age approached. In particular I would like to thank: Belinda my wife, who accepts my crazy goals and supports me every step of the way; my children Tom and Ruth, who constantly remind me that I am no longer young; Anne my PA, whose fantastic organizational skills enabled me to work efficiently enough to become free of debt just after my 50th birthday; James my personal trainer, who would not listen when I said 'I don't do running' and within eight months had me completing the London Marathon and actually enjoying the experience! Dennis, my uncle, who is 31 years older than me to the day and whose escapades prove that I can look forward to at least another 31 years of fun; and finally, to Victoria at Hodder who agreed to publish this book and was gentle with me when I overran the copy deadline by three weeks!

about the author

Robert Ashton was born in 1955 and so has experienced the shock of turning 50. He decided to treat it as a milestone rather than a millstone and set out to change his life. Within a year of his big birthday he had paid off his mortgage, run his first marathon and written this, his sixth book.

Robert lives with his family in a converted barn in rural south Norfolk. As well as writing, he works with both businesses and charities wishing to become more entrepreneurial. He is also a Trustee of Norfolk Community Foundation and holds a number of non-executive directorships.

You can learn more about Robert from his website: www.robertashton.co.uk. He also welcomes reader feedback; his email address is: robert@robertashton.co.uk.

introduction

You can't turn the clock back. With the same certainty that night follows day, your 50s will arrive. Indeed if you're reading this book, they probably already have. What you have to do is grasp the opportunities middle age presents with both hands. Naturally, many of those around you will encourage you to regard 50 as more of a millstone than a milestone, but the reality is different, particularly if you rise to the challenge.

This is not however one of those cheesy self-help books that encourages you to be what you clearly are not. It is more a practical guide to middle life. A guidebook for your 50s, packed with sensible tips and new ideas. At 50 you are in the unique position of having both experience and energy. At 30, you're bursting with energy but are still learning fast as you establish your place in society. At 70, you're a wise old owl, but probably not quite as physically energetic as you are now.

The reality is that at 50 almost anything is possible, providing you take positive steps to make it happen. Here are some reasons for starting right now:

- At 50 most people face at least 25 more active years. In that time you can do an awful lot, but only if you start now. In 10 years time you'll only have 15 left and so on.

- To get the most out of some things, a new career for example, you need many years. You've got that time if you act now.

- It won't get easier and nothing stays the same. Imagine yourself standing on a high diving board. The longer you delay launching yourself off into space, the more frightening it will become.

You'll also have some old habits you want to break. The art of personal development is to take it steadily and one step at a time. If you attempt to revolutionize your life in six months you'll fail. Instead, make a lot of little changes and keep making them. It's like training for a marathon. You start off with a short run, then build your stamina and strength over a long time. In time, what today seems impossible suddenly becomes achievable.

Trevor Baylis, the inventor of the clockwork radio, is a good example of a man who achieved both fame and fortune in his 50s. He spent most of his career as a stunt man, performing feats for television and film. Then one day he saw a television programme about the spread of AIDS in Africa and how difficult it was for the aid agencies to tell people in remote rural communities about safe sex. He decided to do something about it and developed the clockwork radio so that people without an electricity supply could still listen to public information broadcasts.

His invention was more successful than he ever thought possible, becoming a desirable gadget in Europe and the USA as well as making a huge difference in Africa. The challenges he encountered along the way inspired him to start a new business, Baylis Brands, that advises and helps new inventors as they seek to follow in his footsteps and see their new products reach the market.

In fact, the experience of Trevor Baylis is typical. He didn't set out to become a household name, he simply had an idea whilst sitting on the sofa watching television. We all do that don't we? What sets Baylis apart, is that he actually got off the sofa and did something about it. It is that commitment to follow your ideas through that divides those that achieve from those that do not. Naturally there are people and particularly books out there that would have you think otherwise. Perhaps they are in reality trying to sell you something!

If you take a look around your local community, be it the place you work, play or live, you will notice, once you start looking, people who get things done and make things happen. In your 50s you are well placed to make a difference. Here are a few factors that will count in your favour.

- Younger people will assume you know what you're talking about. This is because you were around before they were born.

- Older people will trust you more than they trust young people. When you are really old, the vitality, impulsiveness and verve of the young can be disturbing. At 50, you are likely to move a little more slowly.

- You're more likely to be established with contacts, local knowledge and perhaps even a degree of financial security that others only aspire to.

Of course there is nothing new in all this. What you need to develop is the ability to set your own course through this fascinating decade of your life. You need to be proactive and make positive choices. The alternative is to simply carry on as you are, and make your decisions based on the opportunities that others decide to place in your path.

Within this modest book, you will discover much to excite you as you come to terms with your age. It will help you plan to enjoy almost every aspect of your life, providing you with tips on dealing with everything from student sons to fragile fathers, problems with your pension, relationship issues, and much more besides. It is written for baby-boomers by a baby-boomer and thus is relevant to our generation.

You have taken the first step towards making your 50s special. In fact, you have the opportunity to make these next few years the best of your life.

Action plan

Two heads are always better than one. Take a look at the list of contents of this book with your partner. With her (or his) help, decide which of the topics covered you should explore first. Don't be afraid to re-number the chapters with a pencil, in your own order of importance. Then, start with the most important chapter and begin.

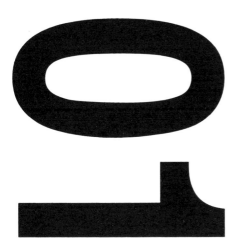

01

enjoy being 50

In this chapter you will learn:
- why 50 is the new 40
- how to act your age without acting old
- the benefit of being 50.

Frankly you have no choice. You are in your 50s and that's that. As with any stage in your life you will find both challenges and opportunities. You have to make the most of what you have and where you are. Looking forward is the best policy. Luckily, at 50 you have a lot to look forward to. It's a great age to be.

Things you can do better now you're 50

So you want to know how to enjoy being 50. It's often described as 'the new 40', which of course is exactly what it is. What you need to do is recognize the benefits of being middle aged and avoid the trap of regarding it as a virtual death sentence.

The myth that 50 is old is a hangover from the early days of the last century. In 1901 average life expectancy in the UK was 47 years! In those days, 50 was indeed old. Today, as a man you can expect to live until past your 80th birthday.

Of course if you really want to be old at 50, you can try eating too much, not exercising at all and smoking 60 cigarettes a day. Each of these is potentially life shortening, but combining all three will make pension planning less of a worry for you. However, let's not go there. Instead let's look at how you're going to make 50 a milestone or turning point in your life.

Why you're taken more seriously at 50

It's important to acknowledge the impact of time on your life thus far. You probably socialize mainly with people of around your age and so it's easy to take your life experience for granted. Reflect on all those things you've done, all those places you've visited and all the things you remember of which today's young people can have little experience.

Even if you've spent the last 30 years standing in the same spot, in the same factory, carrying out similar tasks in your day to day work, you have gained lots of valuable experiences. For one thing you've developed and refined your ability to relate to other people. You've been excited and upset many times and are less likely to be taken by surprise by whatever your world throws in your direction.

Here then are some specific reasons why you're more likely to be taken seriously at 50. More importantly, I'll give you a few tips on each point so that you can make best use of the opportunities each presents.

You look older

Your kids might tease you, but those wrinkles and grey hair give you status in our age conscious society. People make assumptions about us from the way we look; it's human nature to do this. Because you look as if you've been around the block a few times, those you meet will instinctively assume that you can speak with more authority than if you were say 30.

To emphasize this you need to:

- steer clear of trying to disguise your age (no hair dye!)
- dress appropriately, neither like an old man nor a teenager
- have the confidence to develop and follow your own visual style.

You've seen more

Without boring people with stories from your past, it must be acknowledged that you've been around a while. Therefore you have inevitably seen more. Your challenge is to interpret what you've seen before within the context of today's situation. For example, if like me you took your driving test in the early 70s, you'll have had to do hand signals. Today you'd be mad to stick your hand out of the window of a moving car so alas it's a redundant skill. On the other hand, you're probably pretty good at dealing with people in authority, having been raised in a less politically correct era.

To emphasize this you need to:

- recognize that younger people have seen less – and see things differently
- be selective and only share relevant experiences from your past
- make sure you keep yourself up-to-date too.

You're better off

Unless you're really unlucky, you've probably got more wealth now than you had 20 years ago. You probably still have a mortgage but the chances are, you're somewhere on the housing ladder. You've also almost inevitably acquired many of the bits and pieces essential to modern life. Pull open a few drawers and you'll see what I mean. There are things you have forgotten you own that others are still saving for, or more likely, have yet to be given for their birthday.

This relative material wealth translates into an ability to lend things to people. You'd be surprised at how empty some people's garages are and how grateful they'll be if you can lend them the odd bit of kit.

To emphasize this you need to:

- have regular clear-outs so at least you know what you've got
- volunteer to lend people things
- pay your way in the pub.

Gravitas

Gravitas is not a word everyone is familiar with, but it captures the very spirit of being 50. Having gravitas means that you get noticed and command respect. Not yet so old and doddery that you get ignored, you can speak with authority, you have had lots of experiences, both good and bad and you know how to handle yourself too.

You can cultivate gravitas but need to make sure you get the balance just right. Too much gravitas can make you seem arrogant or even pompous. Too little and you'll not make the most of being 50. Here are some ways to 'do gravitas':

- Pause and think before jumping in with both feet to any new situation. Gravitas means you don't react immediately, but when you do it's with good effect.
- Walk don't run. You're an old dog now with plenty of tricks up your sleeve. You can afford to walk as you know where you're heading. Let others duck and dive and dart about.
- Feet on the ground. You don't do panic anymore. You know that time is a great healer and however bad things look right now, in time they'll get better. Of course you move to get things done, but you have the benefit of 50 years life experience. You keep your feet firmly on the ground.

George

Always busy, George didn't notice the years rolling by. He always rushed about and in many ways acted like someone 20 years younger than his age. Then he hit 50.

It dawned on him that he had reached a milestone in his life and needed to change his tactics. He no longer needed to prove himself to everyone; most of the people he knew already thought highly of him.

What was needed was a change in style; a more measured paced approach. He needed to demonstrate his wisdom through thoughtfulness and guile, not by chasing his tail.

George slowed down. His 50s lay before him and he relished the challenges this decade offered. People noticed a change in George. They couldn't quite put their finger on what had changed, but somehow, he seemed to have finally grown up.

Things you're best to avoid at 50

Have you seen the male equivalent of 'mutton dressed as lamb'? I remember one amazing guy of about 60. I saw him sitting outside a coffee shop last summer. He had been on the sun bed to the point of having skin like old tea-bags, flowing hair dyed blonde, a shirt open to his waist and wait for it, a large medallion. He looked so utterly stupid that I looked around for the TV camera. There wasn't one; this guy really did think that he would be seen as a lothario. In fact he looked a fool.

You need to make sure that you avoid looking stupid too. Equally important is to avoid developing the kind of style your father adopted when he was 50. Remember that 30 years ago, 50 was considered old, with the only things to look forward to being a pension and more time to work the allotment (of course, the allotment may still be your chosen hobby, but not necessarily because you're retiring!).

The reality today is very different, but only if you make it different. It is your responsibility and yours alone to take control of the situation and be the person you want to be. You simply need to be yourself.

Look the part

At 50 you have more choice. You get away with dressing like your parents or dressing like your kids. You are bang in between the two. However, as with the earlier example you can also try too hard! Like so many things in life, looking the part means a degree of compromise. You need to strike a happy balance and not be afraid to develop your own individual style.

So, to look the part you need to avoid:

- dressing like your kids or other young people
- dying your hair; grey need not be bad but if you really hate it, be subtle in your colour change and not too noticeable!
- ignoring current trends and steadfastly sticking to your blue blazer and alumni tie.

Accept gravity

There's no point in denying it. As the years roll by your body does begin to sag. Muscle tone is lost and your face in particular will develop wrinkles and folds. Whilst you may be tempted by plastic surgery, or by using Botox™ to fill out those annoying creases, recognize these changes for what they are. If you want to be treated with the respect and deference due to someone who's made it to 50, it's helpful to actually look your age. No amount of surgery can turn back the clock and there's a real danger of losing the very character you're trying to emphasize.

You do however need to adjust your clothes and hairstyle to compensate for these inevitable, but not necessarily alarming physical changes. Chins for example can multiply as the skin under your jaw begins to slacken. Wearing a collar and tie can exaggerate this, making you look somewhat toad like. Luckily business dress today is far less formal and so you have the option in most situations of dumping your tie and loosening your collar. This both feels and looks much better.

Gravity is going to take its toll so avoid:

- squeezing your neck into tight collars
- letting your belly hang over your trousers
- plastic surgery because it shows!

Top tip: Wearing collarless 'granddad' shirts give you the formality of a buttoned up shirt without emphasizing your sagging chin.

Live in the present

Of course you have fond memories from the past. You grew up in an era when the Ford Corsair represented the ultimate in motoring style; you endured the power cuts brought about by the 'winter of discontent' (in the UK) and had parents who smoked. Life in the 1960s was very different to life today, but few young people today want to hear about it.

Of course history is interesting, but not to everyone. To say, 'in my day we did it this way', can to many seem almost insulting. Everybody knows that things change, but when confronted with a challenge, tomorrow's solution is more interesting that yesteryear's.

You memory will also play tricks on you. You may have fond memories of your first car, but in reality, when compared with today's model it was noisier, slower, less economical and less well built. In the 1970s all young men were adept at sanding rust and filling bodywork with glass fibre filler. Today, car bodies are virtually rust-proof. Modern paints have rendered your rust-repairing skills obsolete. You need to forget about it and move on.

Make sure then that you avoid:

- living in the past
- telling people how things used to be better; they usually weren't!
- reminiscing about stuff no one does anymore.

Stay positive

Moaning will get you nowhere. In fact it will lose you friends and impress no one; the one thing worse than living in the past is trashing the present. You are 50 and nothing is going to change that. You are less energetic, less ambitious, less attractive and less tolerant than you were at 20. Or at least that's how it can seem sometimes.

The reality is that whilst you might lust after young women (or young men for that matter) you are also attracted to people of your own age. When you were 20, the concept of sex with someone of 45 would have revolted you. Now it actually appeals and may well represent the reality of your current relationship.

One of the major benefits you have as a baby-boomer is that you are far from alone. There are a lot of us out there and so there's no excuse for ageing alone.

You need to avoid being negative and:

- complaining about your aches and pains
- criticizing people for doing things differently
- seeing being 50 as some kind of disadvantage.

Sometimes, feeling negative or low can turn into depression. One in three people suffer from some form of mental illness at one time in their lives and depression is the most common. If you find yourself feeling down all the time and unable to shake off the blues, talk to your doctor. Depression is easily treatable and there's no shame in admitting you're feeling depressed.

New opportunities that only present themselves at 50

If you keep your eyes and ears open, you'll find lots of new opportunities that just were not around when you were younger. For one thing, old people will take you more seriously now you're properly 'grown up' and younger people will no longer see you as a threat.

A few years ago, people even retired at 50. If you have plenty of years service under your belt with a 'blue chip' employer, this might be an option for you now. For most of us though, being 50 gives us the freedom to challenge the status quo and avoid that once traditional, gradual slide into retirement. After all, you might not want to retire for another 20 years.

Investing

If you've had kids and avoided divorce, you probably find now that your income regularly exceeds your monthly expenditure. You might take this as an opportunity for high living and that's all right. Another possibility is that you will discover the benefits of investing.

The investment world is vast and complex. It is also heavily regulated so it ought to be easy to spot the rogues from the good guys. Your approach to investing your surplus earnings should err on the side of caution; you don't want to risk losing it all.

This book cannot possibly offer you effective investment advice; you need to find an expert you can trust to do that. However, here are some points you might not otherwise consider:

- Paying off your mortgage and owning your home outright gives a huge sense of achievement.
- Investing little and often is easier than saving and then deciding what to do with a lump sum.
- Never act on the spur of the moment. Good investment opportunities rarely demand a snap decision.
- Be wary of friends looking for investment in their business. If the bank's said no, it might be sensible for you to do the same.
- Don't make yourself poor today in anticipation of a comfortable retirement. Make sure you enjoy today as well as save for tomorrow.
- Investing in property at home or abroad.

Maurice

With the children now at work and supporting themselves, Maurice found he had money to spare each month. This hadn't happened since he was a boy! His wife had a good job and he ran his own small consultancy.

He was embarrassed to admit it, but he'd never really had the need to study investments, so didn't really know what to do with the spare cash. He saved it for a few months then started to read the financial pages in his Sunday paper with a little more interest.

Confused, he was introduced by a good friend to an independent financial adviser. The adviser helped him see his financial situation in context. (Retirement was his goal in ten years time.) A low risk investment strategy was developed and Maurice felt much more comfortable. Money is easy to manage when you've not got enough. Too much presents a whole range of new challenges!

If you want to find a good financial adviser or mortgage lender, always shop around. Make sure you pick people that are independent rather than tied to any one insurance company. Also ask for testimonials and don't be afraid to check them out.

Inheriting

Statistically, you are more likely to lose your parents in your 50s than at any other time of your life. We all hope our parents will live for ever, but the sad fact is that you are likely to become an orphan in your 50s. This is perhaps not so much a 'new opportunity' as a tragic inevitability. Aside of the emotional and practical challenges this presents, you are also quite likely to inherit sometime in the next 20 years.

If you've struggled to make ends meet, to give your children a good start in life and to keep debt under control, inheriting can be surprisingly traumatic. For one thing, you might be wrestling with the feelings of guilt that you didn't do more to encourage your parents to spend more whilst they were alive. You are also confronted with more opportunity than you may ever have seen before.

Inheriting opens up a confusing array of options. You might be able to retire; you might decide to take time out to travel; you might want to save money for present or future grandchildren; or you might want to put money away for when your own children need to buy their first homes.

As with any investment, you need to take professional advice, but here are some questions you might ask yourself:

- Do you want the money to change your life or make the life you lead now more comfortable?
- If you don't really need the cash, could you pass it straight on to your children?
- If you're not sure what you want to do, do nothing until you are! Take professional advice. A solicitor is often a good person to ask. Check your locality for one who specializes in family law. Ask around or simply check out on the internet.

Self-awareness

In a world filled with life coaches and others keen to help you connect with yourself, it's easy to be dismissive about self-awareness. However, at 50 you ought to have had time to get to know yourself really well. You've long since survived the crisis of puberty and adolescence. Your values and moral attitudes have probably evolved over time and are now pretty robust and you know your limitations.

Hopefully you will like yourself; that's quite important! Over the years you'll have learned to compensate for your shortcomings and capitalize on your strengths. It's also fair to say that if you're going to have any kind of emotional crisis, you've probably had it by now. You stand at 50 a pretty robust, if battle-scarred man, with a good degree of self-awareness.

What you may have overlooked is how to use that self-awareness to your advantage. It stands to reason that if you've taken 50 years to get to where you are, others younger than yourself are still making the journey. You need to appreciate that others will be less self-aware and perhaps less self-confident than you are. Even if outwardly, they look very confident indeed. Here are some things you are likely to be good at as a result:

- **Listening.** People tend to confide in older people. They unconsciously assume that with age comes wisdom. Your own urge to 'score points' and jockey for position has probably faded, so you have the opportunity now to be a good listener. More importantly, you need to work at knowing how to give effective feedback. Sometimes, feedback is not needed and you can probably feel when that is the case.
- **Encouraging.** We're always being encouraged to set goals and measure our performance against others. As an older person

you can credibly encourage younger people to stretch themselves in whatever field they choose.

- **Keeping secrets.** People will confide in you more as you grow older. This is because they see you as someone non-threatening, with experience and life skills. You have to respect those confidences and not blurt out the things that people tell you.

If you feel you need to work on your self-esteem, here are three simple things you can do:

1 List the barriers to happiness you've overcome through your life.
2 List the things you feel are holding you down right now.
3 Use the solutions you've already tested to work on your current challenges.

Remember that every living person has self-doubts and concerns. We all feel that others are somehow better prepared than we are to cope with everyday life. The fact is, we are all the same. Some just cover their feelings of insecurity better than others.

Challenge ageist beliefs

At 50 you can challenge the way others view mid-life. It's not about slowing down, getting fat, giving up and becoming a bore. At 50 you still have the potential to compete at sports, succeed at study, start a new career, be amazing in bed and much much more. All you have to do is take inspiration from this book, set yourself some tough goals, get off the sofa and actually do it!

Of course you might not want to revolutionize your life. Mid-life can be really comfortable without major change. If you're happy where you are, think about how even quite small changes might make your life even better.

Some encouraging case studies

We all need heroes. When you reach 50 it's good to find some new, older heroes. These will differ markedly from those people you admired earlier in life. Few will be footballers, racing drivers or entrepreneurs. After all, the leaders in those fields are in all probability younger than you!

At 50 you want heroes you can strive to emulate. Ideally these will be people older than you who have yet to embrace the failings of old age and continue to set the pace. It's also fair to say that as a man, your heroes will also be men. In fact, women of our age often have quite different aspirations, but I guess you've spotted that already! (If you're a woman reading this you may be interested to know that a sister title, *Teach Yourself Life at 50 – for Women* is also available and tailored to your specific needs.)

What is also interesting is that some of those we admired in our youth are still achieving today. They've managed to maintain their lead, to ignore the fact that they're getting old and simply keep doing the business. For example, Cliff Richard and Paul McCartney are still singing at 64 and have been part of the popular music scene for almost all of our lives.

Your heroes need not be famous. All they have to do is have some attribute you admire and hope to retain when you reach their age. I can remember attending a men-only dinner and sharing a table with two men in their 70s. For some reason, the subject of sex came up. One of the two, John, admitted that he and his wife still enjoyed a healthy sex life. In fact they often went to bed for an hour in the afternoon. The other man was less fortunate. Cliff commented that health problems had rendered him impotent several years ago and for him sex was now a fast-fading memory.

Most of us will want to be virile like John, but others may already be encountering problems. If you're not happy with your sex life, consider discussing it with your doctor.

Other older people I admire and seek to emulate include Ron. Ron is in his early 60s and a coach at the local running club. He's been running for years and his body has not developed that all too common paunch. What really makes Ron a hero is that he can run faster than I can, for greater distances than I can. He's outperforming people 20 years younger than he is at an age when many of his peers are complaining about aches and pains and rarely walk if they can avoid it, let alone run! I want to be able to run like Ron when I'm 60 and am training hard to catch up with him.

Andy

Andy is a real person. His story is tinged with sadness but is by no means unusual. Andy chose to radically change his life in his early 50s and it is for that reason that his experience is described here.

Born in England, with a typical provincial upbringing, Andy left school to become an apprentice at the local printing works. Over the years he progressed up through the organization, got married, had two children and lived the kind of life millions of us live.

Night school and part-time university study enabled him to join the bottom of the management ladder and by the time he reached his late 40s, he was running the firm. Responsible now only to the family that owned the company he increasingly found himself at odds with their vision of the future. He wanted to build the business and they were more interested in taking out the profits for themselves.

Then tragedy struck. His eldest son was killed in a road accident. This horrific event forced Andy to take a fresh look at his life and how he was spending it. He resigned from his job and set himself up as a freelance consultant, working with family firms facing the same challenges of growth that had confronted his former employer.

Coincidentally, Andy started working for himself at the age of 52. Hopefully you won't need such a traumatic event to prompt you to take stock of your life and how you're spending it.

George

As 50 approached George decided that it was time to take control of his body. He'd always had an athletic build, but his father had put on a lot of weight in mid-life and then died at 55 of a heart attack. George did not want to follow in his father's footsteps.

He'd always exercised after a fashion and went to the gym a couple of times a week. He had slipped into a comfortable routine that kept him reasonably fit, but didn't push back any boundaries. However, he wanted to make 50 memorable and the decade that followed special.

George hired a personal trainer. James was 21 and relished the opportunity of knocking George into shape. He would not take no for an answer and pushed and coerced George to take up all kinds on new activities, including competitive running.

Within eight months of his 50th birthday George ran the London Marathon. He also now does weight training and has joined a running club. He has explored miles of quiet country lanes around his home and has a number of routes mapped out for his training runs.

Now 51, George has never been fitter. His next project is to visit an image consultant, tip out his old wardrobe and try new clothes. There is now no holding George back! (Fitness is dealt with in Chapter 03.)

Once you start looking, you find countless men that have taken up new interests at 50. It can be the most liberating age for many. For example:

'I enjoyed my 50th birthday immensely; we partied 'til dawn.'

Edward

'I don't care what people think, I'm going to do it anyway.'

Keith

'I finally managed the full lotus position a few months ago.'

Stuart

'At 50 you can admit to not being as wise as you thought you once were.'

Steve

'I returned to the classroom as a student shortly after my 50th.'

Paul

These are just a few examples that illustrate the range and breadth of challenges people accept at 50. You cannot deny the fact that you've lived for half a century, but you can demonstrate that you're a long way off being old!

Action plan: how to act your age without being middle-aged

How do you strike the right balance between acting your age and making the most of life at 50? Here are some tips to set you on the right track:

- **Flatter folk.** At 50, younger people expect you to know the answers and may defer to you. Respond by making a point of giving them the credit for having good ideas. They'll think all the more of you for it.
- **Look the part.** If you need help striking that happy balance between dressing like your son or your father, seek advice.

Image consultants aren't cheap, but worth every penny. Ask for a makeover for your next birthday.

- **Smile and enjoy it.** Life's good if you make it that way. Steer clear of cynicism and try not to complain. Smile and others will smile with you.

- **Think of your strengths.** At 50, you're in a strong position. You've the maturity to understand and the youth to act. Most wealth in the world belongs to people aged over 50. You may be better off than you think.

- **Look around you.** Don't listen to the advice of those who want to hold you back. Find people your age who inspire you and follow their example.

This first chapter has introduced you to the notion that 50 is OK. Being considered middle-aged is an asset not a threat. You've a whole world to explore and are probably better qualified, equipped and prepared now than you ever have been and ever will be. Grab every opportunity that comes you way and make your 50s the finest decade of your life.

02

planning your 50s

In this chapter you will learn:
- how to set life goals
- how to find more time
- how to set priorities.

Setting priorities and goals

It may be years since you last stopped to set some goals for your life. Perhaps you had grand plans as an idealistic young man, or perhaps your head was full of other things. Life quickly seems to take over and before you know it, years have passed by.

That's not to say that those years have been anything but happy. You have had work to occupy your mind, with the pleasures that come from an evolving career. Couple this perhaps with relationships and maybe children, and you can see how time can rocket by.

Now as you contemplate 50, from whichever side of that milestone you happen to find yourself, it's time to take stock. It's time to think of yourself, rather than making too many sacrifices. It's also time to look forward.

What confronts you might at first seem daunting. You have to accept that at 50 you are no longer young and getting old is far from appealing. You need to remember that 50 is not actually old. Retirement at 65 is no longer compulsory and anyway that age is 15 years away. That's as long as it probably took you to grow from birth to your first proper shave!

You do not however have to let these next few years pass unchallenged. The goals you set and the plans you make will literally shape the rest of your life. You are also probably better equipped now for the opportunities you choose to face. With maturity almost inevitably comes experience. Wisdom and wrinkles are often closely linked!

Finding your starting point

Before you can plan your future, you need to work out where you are. It sounds obvious but actually isn't. You may have been too busy to notice your life journey thus far. What's more you might not have recognized quite how much you've achieved so far. Here is a simple process you can follow to work out where you are with your life right now. Simply fill in the table, or copy it if you think you'll need more space.

	what's really good	what's not so good
health and fitness		
relationships		
work		
income		
savings		
your home		
free time		
learning/skills		
any other 'hot topics'		

You may find you need to do some research to complete this. In fact, I'd recommend you do. It's not good enough to simply write that you're not happy with something. You need to be able to spell out why. For example, if you're not satisfied with your income, you need to understand why. Not having enough is not going to be a clear enough answer when it comes to setting some goals for the future. In other words you need to work out:

- how much money you have coming in each month
- how much you're spending and on what
- what it is you'd buy if you had more (or perhaps save)
- how large the gap is between what you want and what you have.

This exercise is of course easier with money than in some other areas. For example, if you would like your relationships with those close to you to be better, you need to put your finger on exactly what it is you feel is missing. Perhaps you want sex more often than your partner, or wish your children showed you more respect. The more specific you are in identifying the good and not so good aspects of your life, the easier goal setting will be.

Dealing with things you want to change

No two men will have exactly the same mix of good and not so good things. Just as your life thus far has evolved to become a unique mix of experiences, so too will your future differ from the man standing beside you.

After some of the sacrifices you may have made in the past, for example raising a family, thinking of yourself might not come easily. Once you become accustomed to the idea that one benefit of getting older is greater freedom, making changes can actually be quite fun.

Here are some questions to ask yourself as you plan:

1 Which of the 'not so good' areas are most important to you?
2 What are the barriers to you changing them straight away?
3 Are some interlinked? If so, which will need dealing with first?
4 How will I feel when I've changed some negatives into positives?
5 What do I want my life to look like in five and ten years time?

By starting with the things that you know you want to change, you should be able to make space to see further ahead. In reality, some of today's niggles might simply disappear as you move closer to your longer-term objectives.

How to set goals for the rest of your life

Setting long-term goals are what this is really about. It's too easy to get wrapped up in today's traumas and forget the bigger picture. To set some goals for your future, you need to write them down. Here are some ideas to stimulate your thinking:

- Peter wants to ride a motorbike coast to coast in the USA.
- Hazel wants to write a best-selling novel.
- Mohamed wants to travel the world.
- Nadine wants to start a business importing ethnic African art.

It might be that your long-term hopes and ambitions have been pushed to the back of your mind by everyday life. Now is the time to open your mind and let them flood back.

To make them real, you need to write them down. Do this in the present tense, but set in the future. For example:

- It's 14 February 2010 and I am enjoying my 60th birthday astride a Harley Davidson. Tonight I will arrive in Las Vegas.

  Peter

- It's 20 August 2020 and my 65th birthday was made really special when the postman brought the cheque for £500,000 from the firm that has just bought out my company.

  Nadine

Having written your ultimate goal in this way, you can then work back and write down the intermediate goals that will get you there.

People you might consult and places you might go in search of inspiration

You're determined to enjoy being 50, yet somehow inspiration is not striking. Perhaps you've been too dutiful for too long and neglected thinking about yourself. Or perhaps you're facing a bewildering range of choices, all of which appeal but not all of which are possible.

The answer to this conundrum is not to try to tackle it on your own. Because the subject of your thinking is you, it's pretty much impossible to be objective and rational. Emotions, both positive and negative, will creep in and scupper your thinking. You may need the help of those around you to choose the best opportunities for you.

There are plenty of people who can help you plan to make the most of this decade. Many of them appear again later in the book, as we explore key areas in more detail, but right now you're setting priorities.

Partner

The person you share your life with is probably the person who knows you best. She or he will be highly qualified to discuss your ideas and perhaps even suggest some of their own. Sometimes your partner's suggested goals are more daring than those you'd think of yourself!

Discussing with them how you are going to make the most of being 50 is a good place to start. It's likely in fact that you're similar in age and so you can trade suggestions and feedback. Some goals might be shared ones; things you're both hoping to do.

Why not spend your next holiday away together planning to make your 50s special?

Children

If you have children, they are probably going to be old enough to have some pretty firm views about you and your life. Give them credit for being able to offer you sensible suggestions, as well as for knowing how to wind you up. Ask your children what they feel you should do to make this decade special and listen to what they say. Of course some ideas will benefit them as much as you, but that's OK. It might suit you anyway!

Parents

You've probably spent half your life not listening to their advice. Why not seek it now? They may be getting on a bit but they have survived their 50s and may have some experiences that will help you. As with your children, beware that the advice offered may be a little biased. Accept too that it's usually well intentioned and therefore worth listening to.

Friends

Are your friends also reaching their half centuries? Have a party and use the evening to compare notes. It's surprising how well you can know someone yet not have discovered their secret ambitions. Compare ideas, priorities and see how varied they are. It could be that some of you share goals. You might plan to achieve them together. (Remember that motorcycle ride across America? It would be much more fun with a friend!)

Your boss

It sounds strange, but your boss might have some really good ideas for your 50s. Yes, one of them might involve early retirement, to make way for someone younger, but that's doubtful. As you consider how to make the most of this decade, your boss is worth a mention. Many employers are rather slow at communicating their plans with the team. Asking the questions yourself can draw all kinds of opportunities into the open.

One specific topic to raise with your boss is the way you might work together to plan a staged retirement. Don't panic, this is not an invitation to consider retirement when you are so young, more an opportunity to make sure your boss's expectations are managed.

Your heroes

We all had our childhood heroes, they've been mentioned before. Your choice of heroes will have changed over the years, but sometimes it's worth researching your early heroes to find out how they handled mid-life. You may be surprised by what you discover.

Often, people who achieve a lot in their youth find it really difficult to cope with mid-life. Others simply take on new challenges and remain in the public eye. Many successful people re-invent themselves every few years. In some ways, by setting new goals you may be doing the same.

Everyone else

People watching is a fascinating pastime. Not as intrusive as nosiness, it's more about being observant and noticing what other people are doing. For example, you might be in a restaurant and notice a large and noisy party on another table. At the table is a man a little older than you, clearly at one with himself and enjoying life. He looks comfortable, appears to be at the centre of his group and to be really enjoying the evening.

The reality of his situation might be very different from your perception. That does not matter. It is how the scene looks that sparks your interest and gets you thinking. Sometimes, as you casually observe, you can build a very specific picture in your mind of the other person's life. As you almost role play the life you think they lead, you can get a much clearer perspective on the things you want to do yourself.

Retreats

You don't have to be religious to go on a retreat. Retreats are simply places you can go to escape the day-to-day and think about your future. A retreat can be as simple as an afternoon in your garden shed with 'do not disturb' on the door. Equally, it might be an organized week-long sojourn at some tranquil place.

Many religious communities offer retreats (you do not need to be actively practising that religion to join one). If you simply want to focus on yourself and not be drawn into group activity, look out for what are called 'unsupervised retreats'. These are where you can enjoy the peace and quiet and not be expected to do anything.

Sometimes though, it can be good to take part in activities you would not normally consider. 'Organized retreats' are facilitated to varying degrees. For example, you might find yourself living communally and sharing household chores and tasks. Whilst this may sound daunting, it's a great way to tune into both other people and yourself.

Here are a few retreat ideas to get you thinking:

- a week's solitude in a remote Irish monastery
- camping on your own, high on the moors (in summer!)

- crewing a sailing ship with ten complete strangers
- staying in a guest house on a tiny island, cut off by the sea.

There is an old saying that 'if you do what you've always done, you'll get what you've always got'. In other words, if you're going to make the most of the next few years, you need to change a few things right now to enable you to plan your way forward. Quality time with people close to you, as well as a retreat on your own, can go a long way towards making this possible.

Stepping outside your comfort zone

One of the real benefits of being 50 is that you can get away with almost anything. You're old enough to know better, but also old enough to know when you can push the envelope just a little. However, rather like the budgerigar that refuses to fly out of its cage when the door is left open, you might need a little encouragement.

If you cast your mind back to your adolescence, there were probably lots of things you found really challenging that now you take for granted. For many, asking a girl for a date is perhaps an obvious example. You'd probably find it a lot easier to do today than you did 30 years ago!

Recognizing that your comfort zone has probably expanded over the years will help you to expand it further. The answer, however, is not to put yourself in a very uncomfortable position. This can actually have the opposite effect to the one you are seeking.

Simple starting points

We are all creatures of habit. For example, when you get dressed in the morning, you will put your clothes on in the same order every day. When you shower, you will soap your body in the same sequence each time. These habits develop as short-cuts to save you time and thought. The management writer Edward de Bono once calculated that there were thousands of possible sequences for getting dressed in the morning. If you thought about it, you'd never get downstairs in time for breakfast!

The way to poke little holes in your comfort zone then is to try different things. Even the smallest change can make you more aware of the whole process you are experiencing. For example:

- If you normally wear a tie, try going to work with an open-necked shirt and see how different it feels. You probably won't be the only person dressed this way, unless you work in a strictly uniformed environment.

- Change your route to the shops at the weekend. Make a detour if necessary, but simply travel along an unfamiliar road that is close to your home. Discover things on your doorstep you didn't know were there.

- Make time for breakfast. If your normal morning fare is a latte on the train, get up a little earlier and boil an egg. Experiment with your domestic routine. Some things you'll really hate, but try them all the same.

- Stop yourself saying no. We all say no, sometimes without even thinking. Just because you never have gone to the pub for lunch with colleagues, next time they ask, say yes. (And if they've stopped asking, ask them!) Some of the activities you traditionally shun will actually appeal if you try them now. We all change with time.

Larger steps

Once you've become accustomed to making small changes to your daily and weekly routine, it's time to take some larger steps into the unknown. That is not to say you should take risks. Driving with your eyes closed might take you to a new destination, but it's more likely to get you killed!

The larger steps you take will be things that:

- give you new experiences that will seem strange at first
- you know will only last for a while, then you can return if you want
- have the potential to make your life more interesting, rewarding or worthwhile.

Here are some examples of larger steps you might take that will enable you to try things you perhaps never thought possible a few years ago:

Sing in a choir

The bigger the choir, the easier this is – there is safety in numbers! If you are a confident singer, you might join a small group, but most of us will prefer the relative security of a choir. Clearly your tastes in music will help you make a choice.

What you will find is that once you've overcome the initial embarrassment, you will begin to enjoy the comradeship that results from singing together in some kind of harmony. If singing is definitely not for you, then try some other group activity that encourages you to do something new, alongside other people – take up a new team sport perhaps.

Volunteer

Volunteering is covered in some depth in Chapter 13. For now though, it's good to appreciate that this is one way you can experience the uncomfortable or unusual with the minimum of risk. For example, helping feed and entertain homeless people on Christmas Day will enable you to view your own life from a completely new perspective.

When exploring the outer reaches of your comfort zone, it's important not to make any long-term volunteering commitments. You're experimenting so try to find one-off or infrequent opportunities.

Be someone else

Have you ever swapped lives with someone else? This can be great fun, giving you an insight into the lives other people live. It can also show you how we all tend to make assumptions about people based on what they're doing when we meet them. For example, if you drove a mini-cab on a Friday night in your local big city, you would see a side of life you perhaps would rather ignore. Furthermore, you would be treated very differently too. Being someone else makes it easier to see who you really are.

Of course this might not appeal to you. But, the fact remains that if you're going to make the most of your 50s, you need to shatter a few myths and challenge a few self-perceptions. Abandoning your comfort zone, albeit temporarily, will help you with that no end.

Time management – making time for yourself

There are 24 hours in every day, yet you probably wish there were more. One thing about being 50 is that there's always a lot to do. However, if you're going to make the most of this stage of your life you need to make more time for yourself.

If you have a demanding job, are in a long-term relationship, perhaps have teenage children, a dog, friends, ageing parents and more, then fitting everything into each day will be a constant battle. The trouble is that most of what you do is for others, not yourself. Your family rightly expect your support and involvement, as your employer most certainly does as well. Add in those routine chores, sleep and time with friends and there's nothing left for you.

In your 50s, you need to review the way you spend your time. Are you doing some things from habit and not need? Are you neglecting your own needs to pander to the whims of those around you? Has saying yes become a habit you can't escape from? Then you need to take a look at how you manage your time.

Where does the time go?

Before you can squeeze new activities into your life, you need to see what you can squeeze out. This is the starting point for any time management exercise. It may sound a little like work, but remember the goal here is to help you make more time for yourself.

Get yourself a piece of paper and list down how much time each week you spend:

- asleep (allow eight hours per night even if you usually get less)
- grooming (bathing, shaving, getting your hair cut, etc.)
- travelling (both commuting and those weekend visits to parents)
- working (be realistic, and if you work 60 hours, write it down)
- eating/cooking/household chores

Your table might look like this:

activity	hours per day	hours per week	hours to save
sleeping			
grooming			
eating/cooking/ chores			
travelling			
working			
total			

The right-hand column allows you to note where you think you might be able to free up time without suffering. (For example, sleeping less might save time, but will also make you bad-tempered and less effective.)

These are probably the activities you consider most important, or at least the hardest to give up! Next you need to be honest with yourself and work out how many hours a week you spend:

- watching television
- relaxing (or doing nothing much in particular, for example Sunday mornings in bed)
- socializing

activity	hours per day	hours per week	hours to save
carried forward from above table			
watching TV			
relaxing			
socializing			
grand total			

There are 164 hours in a week. Take your total hours from 164 and see how many you have left. If your total exceeds 164, you will begin to understand why your life seems to be such a rush!

Your schedule might look something like this:

asleep 7 × 8hrs	56
grooming 7 × 1hr	7
travelling 5 × 2hrs	10
working	50
eating/cooking/chores	7
watching TV	21
relaxing	5
socializing (Friday/Saturday night)	8
Total	**164**

This quite logical breakdown of a typical week for a typical 50-year-old man accounts for 164hrs per week. That leaves four hours per week to play with. That's around half an hour a day.

Traffic jams, repairing the washing machine, shopping or even reading this book all eat into those precious four hours per day. Now you can see the size of the challenge. If you're going to have more time for yourself, you need to move some things out of your schedule.

How to save time

You could decide to be a martyr and give up television, or sleep less, or become a clock-watcher at work. In reality though, you know that these are not sustainable. You work long hours because there's a lot to do and you're committed to your job. You need your sleep and television, well what would you talk about at work if you'd missed the show everyone's discussing.

The art of saving time is to make small cuts not large ones. It's also about doing things once and not twice. The biggest incentive to save time is to have something you really want to do with those hours you free up. Here are some top tips that will help you save time:

- **Write things down.** Use a diary to book time for what's important or pin notes on the wall. Don't rely on your memory.
- **Do things once.** If you bank online you can pay your bills when they arrive, scheduling the payment for when it's due. This takes far less time than filing the bill away and then paying it later by cheque. When stuff comes in the post, open it then either act on it or bin it. Don't simply make a pile on the kitchen table.
- **Don't aim for perfection.** Life's not perfect so don't spend hours labouring over every last detail of each task. Aim to be just ahead of good enough. You'll get more done that way.
- **Learn to say no.** The more you say yes the more you get asked to do. It's a simple fact of life. Over time, saying yes becomes a habit. Experiment with saying no.
- **Ask yourself questions.** Television might be an all-consuming passion, or it might simply be that you walk in, switch on, sit down and time just passes. Try watching specific programmes rather than just pick the best of what's on. Record things you want to see and watch them when it suits you.

Setting priorities

The final stage of managing your time more effectively is to set priorities. You need to be sensible about this. Don't, for example, cut down on your sleep to make more time for work. You'll only end up tired and unproductive. When setting priorities you need to ask yourself:

- is this task going to help me achieve my personal goals?
- could someone else do it just as effectively?
- does it actually need doing at all?

You may also find that certain times of day suit certain tasks. For example, some people like to visit the gym first thing in the morning; others prefer to go after work. The same applies to everything you do to some extent. You may prefer sex in the morning to the evening, or of course you may prefer both!

Try to schedule your daily activities so that you do things when you are most likely to be efficient, effective and above all else, enjoy what you are doing.

Action plan: what's important to you and why?

We've asked some fundamental questions in this chapter. What are your goals, ambitions and hopes for the future? What do you want life to look like as you move through your 50s? How can you make time for what really matters to you?

Life gathers momentum from the moment we are born. By your 50th birthday, it's flying along with little time to spare for anything but the essentials. However, you are now beginning to question just how essential some of those activities are. We all tend to add new things to our lives but rarely drop what we're doing already.

Here's how to make it happen for you!

SWOT analysis

This is usually a business activity, where you look at an organization's strengths, weaknesses, opportunities and threats. It applies just as well to your life. Use the list you prepared earlier in this chapter of what's really good and what's not so good to identify your strengths, your weaknesses, the opportunities you face and what threatens your plans for the future.

Doing this exercise will help you check the reality of the goals you have started to set. For example, if debt is a real threat to you, it will inhibit any new activity that costs money. On the other hand, if you've just inherited money, you might be able to cut back on work to make more time for you. Above all else, your plan needs to be realistic if it's going to succeed.

Ask around

You're not going to change your life on your own and nor should you try to. We are all interdependent on one another and so any change to your life will impact on others. Make a list of the people you think might help you make the most of your 50s. If necessary, also make a list of the people you think might try to hold you back.

As you plan your year, also spend some time reviewing your life. It will seem odd at first, but is important all the same. You could try a retreat, or simply take your partner away for a weekend, together with a notebook and pen. Don't try to do too much when you first try this. It takes time to get the hang of reviewing what is probably quite a complex life.

Take some risks

If you're going to do things differently, it makes sense to start practising now. There's a lot to be said for temporarily abandoning your comfort zone. However, you don't want to cut off your escape route back. Plan to take some small, perhaps social risks, that will make you slightly uncomfortable and reflect afterwards on your feelings. How did the reality compare with your expectations? How were you surprised and by what?

Use the list given earlier in this chapter to stimulate your imagination, then be brave and do some things that you wouldn't normally try.

Make time

It's easy to say you've not got the time. You've probably had years of practice at this. However, use the techniques and tips here to free up some time to push back the boundaries of your life. Your 50s are a decade when you should be finding time for new things, not simply trudging along the familiar, well-worn path.

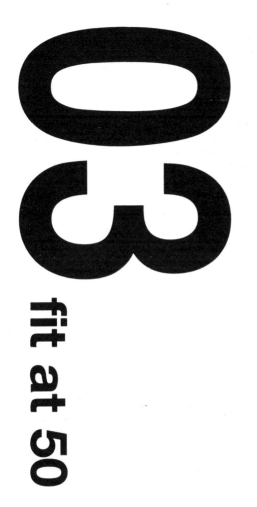

03

fit at 50

In this chapter you will learn:

- how your body changes at 50
- how to improve your fitness
- how to improve your diet.

Many people who have never really been sporting suddenly discover fitness at 50. It doesn't matter if you're sporting a spare tyre, or have the physique of a coat hanger, you can change your body shape, and get fit at 50.

However, if you have any concerns at all about your weight or health, consult your doctor *before* making any changes to you diet or taking up exercise.

Why you need to work harder at being fit

It's never too late to start getting fit. But please don't take this as an excuse to put it off any longer. At 50, the inexorable process of ageing begins to accelerate. The things that kept you fit at 40 won't be good enough to keep you fit at 50. In many ways, you need to exercise harder if you are to stave off an uncomfortable old age.

Let's start by challenging your perception of old age. There were eight men aged 80 or over who completed the 2006 London Marathon. The fastest of these, Peter Addis, covered the 26.2 miles in a respectable 4 hours 53 minutes. At 80, Peter is probably older than your father! Who says you can't be a competitive athlete in old age? The way to do it is of course to make a start right now!

Alternative, less strenuous but equally rewarding goals to aim for could include:

- completing a sponsored cycle ride
- taking a walking holiday in the mountains
- playing football with your children.

Physical changes that occur when you pass 50

Remember that exercise builds up your muscles and even your bones. This is especially true of your heart and lungs. You can also increase your flexibility and remain sexually active if you look after your body.

These are the things the scientists tell us are likely to change:

- **Shrinking muscles.** Every ten years, after middle age you will lose around 3 kg of muscle mass a decade. That might not sound much, but over half a lifetime it adds up to quite a lot.

- **Reducing bone density.** Old people break bones more readily because bones become less dense and more brittle as you age. This decline starts at around 40.
- **Hearts are muscles.** The last place you want to lose muscle mass is from your heart. The good news is that running it up to 70 per cent of your maximum heart rate (220 less your age) for a few 20 minute bursts a week helps keep it in good shape.
- **Fat sticks.** For a variety of reasons, some metabolic and some just lifestyle, it's harder to manage your weight as you age. We chaps tend to get fat around our tummies and this is not good for the organs it surrounds.

You also need to be aware that your risk of certain health problems also increases after the age of 50. Perhaps best known of these is your prostate gland, which can enlarge and even become cancerous. The risk of heart problems is also greater in your 50s, particularly if you are overweight or smoke. It can be sensible to have a thorough medical when you reach 50. Many private health clinics provide these, as of course can your own doctor.

As you advance into this important decade, you need to be more vigilant, without becoming paranoid, and make sure any worrying symptoms are quickly seen by a healthcare professional.

Slowing the effects of time

Any reasonable amount of exercise, even walking the dog, will make a difference. The point to note here is that as age reduces your physique, so exercise can build it. This is true at any age. It's true to say that your potential maximum performance at 50 will be lower than it would have been 30 years ago, but it might well prove to be higher than your actual level of fitness at 20.

Life gets in the way

The trouble with middle age is that you spend more time sitting down. Successful careers mean less running around and more sitting in meetings. Even if you've spent your life on the factory floor, there's less physical work now that health and safety regulations and greater mechanization have made life easier for us all.

Food is also relatively cheap, the house warm and the television churns out programmes from umpteen channels. No wonder we spend our leisure time rooted to the sofa! There have probably never been so many reasons for not staying fit.

Warning signs

You do need to be sensible if you're going to work on improving your body. It's not wise, for example, to go from being a complete couch potato to a gym freak in two months. You need to pace yourself, to take medical advice if you have any doubts or fears, and remember the golden rule: the way to avoid starting something you can't maintain is not to start too much!

Easy ways to eat better

There was a time when being portly was considered a sign of affluence. When food was scarce, the man who could afford to eat well was proud to display his wealth round his waist.

Today, of course, society values have changed and slim is the favoured body shape. This is easier to achieve for some than others.

Body shape

In the 1940s, an American scientist defined three distinct body types. Every man falls into one, or maybe overlaps two, of these types. Understanding what is normal for you will stop you worrying about being something your physique simply won't allow.

- **Endomorphs.** These are the people you might politely call chubby. They tend to be big boned with large limbs and a tendency to put on weight easily. Endomorphs can build muscle, but with it comes fat. Wrestlers are often endomorphs.

- **Mesomorphs.** These lucky people have a naturally athletic build. They look well proportioned and if they take up sport, are usually quite good at it. They can put on weight in mid-life and need to work at keeping in shape.

- **Ectomorphs.** These are the people who can eat a tub of ice cream a day and never get any fatter. Naturally skinny with modest muscles, ectomorphs often want to bulk up their body and feel they look too thin and wimp-like.

The message here is that you need to acknowledge your body shape and recognize that you can't change it out of its natural form. When we reach 50, these differences in body shape may have been magnified by life; the differences will be more pronounced!

What to eat

There are countless books and articles published about diet. Many isolate one component of our diet, say fat, and highlight the dangers it can pose. The reality is that if you start with your instinct, you won't go far wrong. Diet is just one element in the healthy living mix. Furthermore your body shape will also influence your diet. For example:

- **Endomorphs:** often want to lose weight and so watch their consumption of refined carbohydrates, such as sugar. Higher fibre, lower fat foods will also help them match their intake to their energy need.

- **Mesomorphs:** will be pretty laid back about their body and their diet. If they are training, then eating plenty of protein will help them build muscle.

- **Ectomorphs:** often want to put weight on and so eat anything. In fact some specialists will advise ectomorphs to eat all the sugary foods that the endomorphs reject. Sweet fatty foods (such as ice cream) are very palatable because they are very effective.

When to eat

There is no doubt that breakfast is the most important meal of the day. It's also the one most likely to be passed over as we rush to start the working day. A latte and muffin on the way to work is not necessarily the best way to start the day. Aim for fruit and fibre as this will stave off those urges to snack through the morning.

In general, it is best to eat regularly and not simply graze. That's not to say you should sit down for three meals a day; rather that you should have a routine that you know meets your needs and enables you to manage your food intake effectively. Snack and junk foods are what you really want to avoid.

Top diet tips

Your body shape, lifestyle and personal tastes will largely dictate your diet. However, there are some things that will help everyone to eat better and more healthily. They are:

- **Eat breakfast.** Always start the day with something to eat. Ideally, avoid processed or high sugar foods. Go for slow release carbohydrates such as brown bread and muesli.
- **Snack on fruit.** Why not put a fruit bowl on your desk at work? Snacking on fruit is better for you than biscuits and chocolate bars.
- **Read the labels.** You'll be surprised when you start reading what's in the food that you eat. Get in the habit of reading the label and see how much sugar and fat you are really consuming.
- **Drink water.** There is a lot of debate about the value of drinking two litres of water a day. Some advocate it and other experts scoff. Drinking water though is a good habit to adopt. It's better for you and cheaper than fizzy drinks.
- **Don't clear the plate.** Our parents were brought up with wartime rationing. They will have taught you to always clear the plate. Stop eating when you're full and give the scraps to your dog. It'll be better for you both!

Because in mid-life you are more likely to gain weight and develop that spare tyre, you do need to look harder at what you eat. However, you need to recognize that your body type, the amount which you exercise and many other factors combine to define your ideal diet.

Instinct is important, for it is your body's way of telling you what it wants. Aim to balance your instinct with common sense, plus the knowledge you acquire as you seek to understand what it is you are eating. Above all else, don't become a martyr to your diet. Eat, drink and be happy!

Exercising without going over the top

It's good to treat 50 as a milestone and a reason for changing the things you do. Exercise is one aspect of life you can easily alter. What you have to do is avoid going over the top. Set yourself unrealistic goals and you will struggle to achieve them.

What is exercise?

You might think you know what exercise is, but to be of benefit, you need just the right amount of exertion. Too little and you're wasting your time. Too much and you tire quickly and risk harming yourself.

The heart is the critical organ when it comes to defining exercise. Aim to work out at 70 per cent of your maximum heart rate. To calculate this:

0.7 × (220 – your age) = optimum workout heart rate

As a rule of thumb, this is where you feel warm and a little breathless, but you're still able to hold a conversation. To put it another way, if you take a leisurely stroll through the park, it's not really exercising you. Walk briskly and maintain the pace for a while and you'll soon warm up and reach that target heart-rate zone. Break into a run and unless you are already very fit, you'll soon find conversation impossible.

When you pass 50, a good target to aim for is half an hour's exercise per day. It's also better for you if you can maintain the pace for that time in one session.

Where to exercise

Your local gym is full of equipment designed to work different parts of your body, whilst keeping you at the optimum heart rate. Many exercise bikes, for example, have built in monitors that can, if you wear the right equipment under your shirt, give you a constant readout of your heart-rate.

Another benefit of gyms is that they are usually staffed by people trained to help you work out the right exercise programme for your needs. Choose a gym where you think you'll feel comfortable. Some attract bodybuilders, others people of all ages who simply want to get fit.

Many gyms run courses or have allocated schedules specifically for the 50+ age group – you may prefer to start with these if you feel uncomfortable working out with younger people, as they are tailored to your specific needs. Of course you may be fitter than some of your younger peers already!

There are lots of alternatives such as swimming. If you prefer to exercise alone, then try walking, cycling and working in the garden; all are just as effective.

Weight training is something that too many of us dismiss as being exclusively for the young and vain. In reality it can be the perfect boost for flagging self-confidence. Weight training, if done properly, can give your body greater definition. Acquiring more distinct pectorals, biceps and broader shoulders will make you look and feel really good (especially when you compare your physique with men much younger who have perhaps let themselves go!).

Wherever you choose to exercise, the most important thing to remember is to get familiar with that feeling of being short of breath but still able to enjoy a chat. Even climbing the stairs, or walking the dog can then become part of a planned exercise regime. Keep it simple.

When to exercise

Each of us is different so will feel more energetic at different times of the day. As well as making the most of opportunities to exercise as part of our everyday activities, there is also the challenge of squeezing time for exercise into what is probably a very full life.

Exercise can do more for you than make you fit. Going for a brisk walk at lunchtime also clears your head and enables you to reflect on those work challenges. You can then return to your desk refreshed and inspired.

Some people make exercise a social activity. They may join a running club, do a weekly aerobic class or play squash with their boss. Making exercise part of your social life can make it a lot more enjoyable. Salsa classes and yoga are also excellent options for getting fit and de-stressing.

Becoming more flexible

As well as losing muscle mass as you get older you also become less flexible. The good news is that you can easily improve your flexibility by stretching. Athletes often stretch their muscles before a race and almost always stretch afterwards. Ask about stretching at your local gym, or check out some stretches on the internet. If you haven't been able to bend over and touch your toes for years, stretching might bring them back within reach. You might also try yoga: it's a great way to learn how to make your body more supple and flexible.

Reasons for exercising

In case you need some additional encouragement to start exercising, here are some good reasons for doing so.

- **It makes you feel good.** Exercise encourages your brain to release endorphins. These compounds create a feeling of well-being.
- **It's good for your heart.** It's thought that lack of exercise is a major contributory factor in at least one-third of heart attacks.
- **It strengthens your bones.** One in twelve men develop osteoporosis in later life. Exercise strengthens bones and delays osteoporosis.
- **Make love tomorrow.** Strong erections depend on a good cardiovascular system. Keeping your heart in good shape and your sex life will last longer into old age.
- **Keep your balance.** Exercise, and stretching in particular, keep you supple at a time in life when it's easy to lose mobility.

Gym classes used to be called 'keep fit'. As you can now see, you don't need to go to a class to keep fit. You just need to keep active and work a little at raising your pulse for a few hours every week. It's not unusual for men to be fitter at 50 than they were at 30. Will we be able to say that about you in six months' time? I hope so!

Bad habits and how to break them

One man's bad habits are another's virtuous acts. Before worrying about bad habits, you do need to make sure they really are bad. Clearly you need to avoid breaking the laws of the land or the moral codes of society, but what actually constitutes a bad habit?

At 50, you've probably long since come to recognize that many of the bad habits your parents chastised you for, are not really that bad. In fact, some were probably more a projection of their own inhibitions and views than actually likely to do you any harm.

A bad habit then, is simply something you do that you rather wish you didn't do. It might be something that you know harms your health, wastes money, upsets your partner or simply bothers you. Let's be honest, if you've bitten your nails for 40 years they won't drop out if you carry on. Unless you want your hands to look nicer, it doesn't actually matter if you keep on chewing.

Working out the habits you want to break

I'd advise you against asking your family and friends to help you with this task. The resulting list might be too long for anyone to manage! You also need to realize that some habits are only bad if others spot you indulging in them. (Picking your nose is a good example!)

Pour yourself a nice cold beer, take a piece of paper and pen and start writing. Here's a table that you might even choose to fill in:

harms my:	habit 1	habit 2	habit 3	habit 4
health				
pocket				
relationship				
career				
image				

Now add in the four habits you most want to give up and tick the boxes where that habit impacts on the aspects of your life listed on the left. Some bad habits, such as smoking, might cause you to put a tick in every box. Others, such as biting your nails, may only affect your image.

You can use the completed table to set some priorities and work out what you want to change. This is the point where you might choose to involve those close to you.

How to break a bad habit

First, you have to work out why you do it. Stress, for example, is frequently cited as a reason for smoking. If this applies to you, you need to deal with the stress before dealing with the habit. Otherwise you will simply put yourself under more pressure and stress. That's not the way to break bad habits!

Furthermore, there is a danger that you will simply switch one habit for another. Many people who stop smoking put on weight. This is because they replace cigarettes with sweets. Here are five steps to breaking a bad habit:

1 **Be realistic.** Don't take on lots of things at once. Work out what you want to change and focus on that. Set yourself a goal and aim for it.

2 **Get help.** You might choose to share the task with your partner, or even seek professional help. Don't make it hard for yourself if you know that others can make it easier.

3 **Plan a reward.** Mark significant milestones with a memorable treat. Count down the days or put a picture of your reward where you can see it. Use the promised reward to help you stay on track.

4 **Be competitive.** Find a friend keen to do the same thing. You will have your low points at different times. Carry each other along.

5 **Don't seek perfection.** You're bound to make the odd slip. Don't give up when it happens. Recognize instead that you're simply human and focus on what you're achieving overall.

Making a start

It's easy to turn the page and put off getting started. You might even mark the page and have every intention of returning soon. But the longer you put anything off, the harder it is to get round to doing it.

Deadlines are, of course, a part of everyday life and we all learn to deal with them by waiting until the last minute and then completing the task in a panic. In fact, it has been said that the adrenalin surge that accompanies the feeling you've left something too late can actually help!

With a self-imposed deadline, it's even harder. You need to treat it seriously and actually set it in the first place. Only when you've decided when you're going to finish, can you work out when you have to start.

Reasons we all tend to put off making a start include:

• **Self-doubt.** You spend so much time questioning your ability to carry it off that you never actually start. Deal with this by accepting that you might need a few attempts to get it right. There's nothing wrong with failing and then trying again.

• **Procrastination.** Paradoxically, putting things off can actually make you more tense than if you simply get on and do them. It's rather like piling stuff on your desk rather than filing, responding or ignoring each item. As the pile grows, so does your anxiety.

• **Habits are habits.** Your habit is something you do without thinking. You will catch yourself doing it because you always have done it and, unless you act, probably always will. Try tactics that will make you notice those otherwise automatic actions. For example, put your packet of cigarettes in a sealed plastic bag. The act of having to work harder to get one will remind you of your desire to give up. Another example would be to put the biscuit tin just out of reach. Climbing on a chair to get it down from a high shelf gives you more opportunity to question your need.

When you realize the extent to which our lives are full of habits (for example, you will always put on the same sock first, either left or right, without thinking) you realize why bad ones are hard to break. As with any self-improvement activity, you need to keep it simple, keep it achievable and celebrate every success along the way.

Smoking

One of the most common habits people want to break is smoking. Tobacco is very addictive and so the smoking habit is harder to break than many. The UK National Health Service recommends exploring the following techniques:

- **Acupuncture.** Although no one really knows why it works, having someone (expertly) stick pins in you helps many people kick the habit.
- **Cold turkey.** If you can survive the two to three weeks of shakes and aches, this is apparently the most common way people give up. I guess it helps to have a few friends sharing the experience with you.
- **Hypnotherapy.** Fewer needles here than acupuncture and because you are actually discussing your addiction with someone it's easier to see how it works, even if you cannot recall the conversation afterwards!
- **NRT.** No, this is not something your mum does to improve her mood later in life, but 'nicotine replacement therapy'. It's like smokers' methadone and you need to see your doctor to get some.
- **Zyban™.** This drug acts on the parts of your brain that tobacco stimulates and stops you enjoying or wanting a smoke. It sounds scary but is probably very effective, especially if you don't like needles!

Action plan: write your own health and fitness programme

You should now be ready to take greater control of your physical well-being. As you've seen, after the age of 50 things can tend to slide faster if you don't take better care of yourself. When a man hits 50 he is still very much in his prime. However, the path of life is beginning to get narrow and slippery so you need to focus harder if you're going to stay on course.

Above all else, you need to be realistic in what you set out to achieve with your health and fitness programme. You also need to make sure that the things that might get in the way, such as stress, are dealt with first.

Here then is a five-point action plan to help you create your own health and fitness programme:

1 **Define your starting point.** Look at your life, your diet, your fitness and your physique and work out where you are compared to others. Remember that while you're unlikely to be able to change what nature gave you, you can simply bring your body somewhere closer to its intended state.

2 **Set some goals.** Work out from everything in this chapter what it is you want to change. You won't do it all at once so don't even try. Some activities might be linked. Seeking to lose weight and do more exercise are two goals that will help each other out. Other combinations will work less well together.

3 **Seek encouragement.** Make yourself accountable by telling your partner or friends. Let them keep reminding you to see how it's going. Ask them if they can see the difference if they're not volunteering encouragement. You might also find some encouragement from professionals able to help. (These might include dieticians, fitness instructors, hypnotherapists and more.)

4 **Measure your progress.** Did you monitor your pubescent progress with a ruler? Many of us did. This time though, you're going to do more than simply wait for things to happen. You're going to be making things happen and measuring the impact as you go. From your weight, the number of days since your last smoke, to complicated sports performance measurements. Measure your progress, write it down and if it helps, plot your journey on a graph.

5 **Celebrate success.** Don't belittle your achievement when you finally get there. Celebrate your successes and don't be embarrassed to make it a party. Then set some more goals and start the process over again.

Don't underestimate the difference it can make to your life if you are even a little bit more fit and healthy than you are right now. It's never too late to make a difference to your physical well-being. Try it and see!

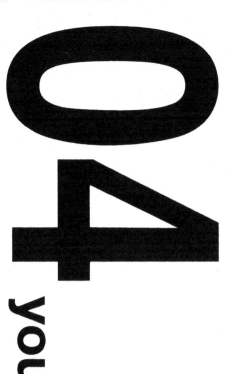

04

your partner

In this chapter you will learn:
- how to improve an existing relationship
- how to have more fun together
- about sex in mid-life.

Energizing a long-term relationship

If you're aged around 50 you're likely to be in a long-term relationship. It might not be your first long-term relationship, but you probably want it to last. Straight or gay, you are probably at a time in your life when you're less likely to want to enter the cut and thrust of courtship all over again.

If, on the other hand, you are not in a long-term relationship, this section can help you find a new partner. If you're happy on your own, and many are, then simply skip this section and move on.

The trouble with a long-term relationship is that you become familiar with each other. This might not seem like a problem, but it certainly can become one. Over time you assume you know what each other is thinking and communication becomes more guesswork than conversation.

However, just as you are no longer the person you were at 25, nor is your partner. She or he has also evolved, grown, developed and changed over the decades. People say they grow apart. This is more that they've failed to grow together. Nothing stays the same, especially a relationship.

What goes wrong

You started your adult life with ambitions, dreams and hopes. Time and experience have changed those goals. You might have discovered that the reality of what you sought is different from the perception you had. More likely, you've got tied up in the week-to-week routine of work and domestic life.

In middle age, repairing the dishwasher can seem a more important priority than taking a walk together, hand in hand, in the park. For one thing you probably loathe washing-up, and persuade yourself that you can easily go for a walk tomorrow instead. Then tomorrow comes and it rains, so you go to your local shopping mall instead. There's little romance in shopping.

Children soak up your time and energy as well. They also get in the way of romance. It really is a case of 'not in front of the children' and even the slightest display of affection, a peck on the cheek for instance, will prompt a loud cry of 'yuk' from your kids.

Conversely, when the children leave home, the vacuum it leaves can create challenges of its own. You have more time together than you've perhaps had for a long time. Not every couple find that easy.

Because you both have lots of other things to do and worry about, you stop making time for each other. Your conversations are about everyday issues and challenges, with your relationship increasingly taken for granted. It really can be as simple as that.

Putting it right

First you have to both accept that a long-term relationship is what you want. Sometimes the grass may seem greener on the other side of the fence. This is however not always the case. You both need to commit to making your relationship work.

Your parents' relationships might influence your thinking here. Did they row all the time? Were they really happy? Do you really know how they felt? Probably not; and anyway, you are not your parents. Your relationship is different in many ways.

Here then are some specific tips to help you re-energize your relationship:

- **Love yourself first.** If for whatever reason you're not happy with your own life, it's unlikely you'll be as happy as you might be in your relationship. Understand what's up with you and share the anxiety with your partner. Don't hold them responsible!
- **Respect the differences.** You are different people, with different strengths and weaknesses. Respect that you are probably both better at different things and help each other where you can. It's what you achieve together that's important.
- **Accept compromise.** Some things you won't change, however much you might want to. For example, if you like late nights and your partner prefers early mornings, you both need to recognize and accommodate that difference. Don't try to make your partner just like you. You need them to be different and so do they!
- **Avoid manipulation.** Both partners in a relationship will know the other's pressure points. Manipulation might be easy, but is not the best technique when you want to get your way. Your children and parents might also be tugging you one way or the other. Recognize when you're being manipulated or manipulative and try to stop.

- **Laugh together.** When things go wrong, laugh about it and don't get bitter. You can't change what has passed and coping positively with the consequences as a couple is the best way forward. Never laugh at each other: that's very different and can be destructive.

Communication then is the key to energizing a long-term relationship. Talking, sharing, listening and understanding will see you through the inevitable highs and lows of your relationship.

In the most successful long-term relationships, partners actually grow to be more alike than when they first met. This may appear rather twee, but for those living together this closely, it's probably idyllic.

Making time for each other

It's just too easy to get wrapped up in the day-to-day stuff. You need, more now perhaps than when you were younger, to make time for each other. This is both true if your relationship is long or recently established. Everyday life presents too many distractions.

Why it's important

You only live once and you want to make the most of every opportunity. Your current partner is quite likely to be the person with whom you share old age. Now is the time to have the experiences that will form tomorrow's happy memories.

It's also important to recognize that your relationship needs your combined efforts to make it work. Some people find this difficult, particularly if other aspects of their lives see a lot of change.

Making time for your partner is not about freeing up weeks or days. It's about making time to be together throughout each day of your lives. Creating frequent opportunities to do things together will strengthen the bond between you.

How to do it

Even the smallest changes to your daily routines can create opportunities to spend quality time together. What you have to do is look at how you spend your day and find things you can do together. It really is that simple. Here are some examples:

- **Eat together.** If meals are usually rushed, set aside one or two evenings a week when you will cook and eat together. Also try taking it in turns to enjoy breakfast in bed one morning at the weekend. Eating together is considered by many almost to constitute foreplay.

- **Bath together.** Candles, incense sticks, soothing music, bubbles and even a rubber duck. Find time to relax in the bath together and simply enjoy being together. If your bath is rather small, all the better. You'll enjoy finding space for all those arms and legs.

- **Meet for lunch.** If you both work in town, why not make it a habit to meet for lunch once a week? You'll both feel refreshed by the break and it's more fun than lunch with colleagues or a sandwich at your desk.

- **Take up a hobby.** It doesn't matter what it is, but taking up an interest you can both pursue will give you quality time together. Furthermore the challenge of learning a new skill, sport or pastime will enable you tackle a new challenge together.

- **Early nights.** Sometimes it's nice to go to bed early. Some find this really difficult, but going bed early, even if you're not tired, means you can talk, cuddle and even make love without feeling hurried.

Common interests

You're probably of a similar age and therefore both coming to terms with mid-life. As you explore the many opportunities this exciting stage of your life has to offer, find things you can do together. New, shared interests are great ways to do things as a couple. Often they create opportunities to make new friends too.

Remember that there may well be things you considered years ago and rejected, that will appeal more today. For example, camping with young children might have been too daunting to try, but now you can leave them at home, it's all the more appealing.

Sometimes, one or both of you will have a hankering to try something 'middle aged'. Embarrassment at confessing to such a thing might hold you back. However, if you make it a dare, you're more likely to try it out. Sometimes you can be pleasantly surprised when you experiment with new things.

Time to yourself

Whereas some couples do seem to be joined at the hip, others adopt a more realistic approach to life. Just as you may need to work at finding things you can do together, you also need to find things you can do on your own.

Your parents will have been very happy to develop separate, gender specific interests. Today they may seem like clichés of life in the 1960s, but they did give each partner time alone. There was a time when men tended to go to the pub and women preferred to sew and arrange flowers. Luckily in many ways times have changed. You might want to arrange flowers and you will both go out for a meal or sometimes just a drink.

Do not see separate interests as a threat to your relationship. They can actually enrich it. The opportunity to encourage your partner in something you don't want to do is great, providing of course they are equally supportive of you.

Some couples take this a stage further, taking some holidays together and some on their own. Riding a motorbike across Europe with some mates may well appeal to you, but why insist on placing your partner on the pillion for every bump of the journey?

Managing our time is one of the key challenges most of us face. Making sure there is time for your partner, and for yourself, will make for a happier life. Challenge the habits of a lifetime and see how life with your partner blossoms.

Simple ways to make her (or him) happy

It's the small things that make a relationship successful. Showing your partner that you care, as frequently as possible, will make all the difference. We all like to feel valued and appreciated.

It doesn't matter if your partner is young or old, they will love you all the more if you shower them with nice surprises. Life does become a series of routines and breaking routines is one of the principal routes to greater happiness.

This section of the chapter is here to give you some quick wins. It will also help you make a habit out of treating your partner and hopefully, they will reciprocate and do the same for you. As you work on other aspects of your relationship, it's good to build in some simple things you can do straight away.

Here then are some suggestions:

- **Do the chores.** In most households, chores are shared out equally. However, now and again, do your partner's chore as well as your own. Better still, suggest doing the chores together.
- **Buy flowers.** A few flowers from the supermarket can cost less than the last latte you consumed. Save the big bouquet for a birthday, but buy flowers as often as the urge takes you. Everyone likes being given flowers.
- **Say 'I love you'.** Don't take your partner for granted. Make a point of telling them how much you love them. Do this often and say it as if you mean it. Avoid dramatic 'on one knee' pronouncements. A simple hug is usually enough.
- **Buy underwear.** If you like your partner wearing nice underwear, go out and buy it for them. Spend perhaps more than they would on themselves.
- **Be nice to your in-laws.** Let's face it, we all find our partner's parents challenging at times. Surprise your in-laws from time to time and see how happy it makes your partner.
- **Book a night away.** Holidays can be fantastic, but you can only afford to take one now and again. Book a night in a local hotel, enjoy a nice dinner and let nature take its course. Do this to celebrate special occasions such as birthdays.
- **Change something they don't like about you.** If your beard, favourite scruffy jumper or smelly trainers are cause for complaint, hold out for a while then get rid of them.
- **Make it personal.** Rather than buy a present, why not make one? If that's too challenging, design something and have it made. It needn't be costly, but will be unique.
- **Be spontaneous.** The best surprises are the unplanned ones. You're out together in town and you see something that appeals. Just do it! Sometimes acting on impulse is liberating for you and exciting for your partner.
- **Be grateful.** If your partner surprises you with an unexpected treat, make sure you show your gratitude. Remember that as with every aspect of a relationship, it takes two to make it work.

For some reason we assume that treats and surprises are for children not adults. Even though at 50 you are no longer a child by any stretch of the imagination, you and your partner will still appreciate nice, unexpected surprises. Take the initiative and do something special for your partner today.

Sex in mid-life: the ups and the downs

By the age of 50 you've probably got over most of your inhibitions about sex. Things like masturbation, for example, are no longer associated with guilt, and you've come to know what you like and what you don't. You've also come to terms with your body and, in particular, your penis. Long or short, thick or thin, you've hopefully worked out that it's what you do with it that matters more than what you have.

If, on the other hand, you do have deep rooted inhibitions, you might find it helpful to consider counselling. Organizations such as Relate (UK) are an excellent place to go for impartial support of this kind. You can visit with your partner or on your own. Both can be useful.

More challenging may be your coming to terms with your children becoming sexually active. This can be compounded by your concerns about your own performance. If your own libido is beginning to wane, a house full of young men with high testosterone levels will do little for your confidence, particularly if you know they are indulging in sexual activity under your roof.

Sex of course remains an important part of our lives when we reach our 50s. In fact, clinicians report that some couples continue to make love into their 80s and beyond. Take comfort from the fact that, as with the rest of your body, your sex life may only have reached its mid-way point.

What's normal?

In the 21st century, normal is usually defined as anything you do with yourself or others that does not cause offence, or lasting physical or emotional damage. Or to put it another way, when you talk to sexual health specialists they will admit that little shocks them and even less surprises them.

However, one man's pleasure may be another man's perversion so you should not worry that you're missing out if your repertoire does not include every option. For most men of any age, sex consists largely of straightforward vaginal intercourse. (A fact many women would cite as something of a problem!)

Frequency is something that bothers quite a few people. It's true that in your 50s you're probably making love less often than you did 20 years ago. The average, according to the experts, is three times a week in your 30s and once a week in your 50s. Of course, as with so many other aspects of mid-life, the focus should be on quality not quantity. A bonus of ageing is that orgasm takes longer to reach. You could argue that you still spend as much time at 50 making love as you did when you were far younger. It's just that you no longer can or even want to finish the job in less than a minute!

What can go wrong?

There are a number of problems you may encounter in your 50s. These are not exclusive to this age group, but are probably more common than you might first think. Remember that your doctor or sexual health clinic will be familiar with whatever problems or concerns you have.

Impotence

The inability to achieve or keep an erection is for many men a nightmare scenario. There may also be unpredictability to impotence. One day you can get a really strong erection that does you proud and delights your partner. Another time, for no apparent reason, you can only get half hard, however much your partner tries to help. Worse perhaps are those occasions where it all starts off OK, but somehow you lose stiffness before ejaculation. This is obviously frustrating for you both.

Impotence can be caused by many factors and is said to affect ten per cent of men at some time in their lives. It can be a symptom of serious disease, which is why it's always best to seek medical advice.

Erections are caused by your penis getting pumped full of blood. If smoking or vascular disease has narrowed your arteries, erections are more difficult to achieve. It's all a matter of simple hydraulics. Other causes include depression, or even anxiety caused perhaps by the fact that you're not with your usual partner!

Impotence can be helped by erection-boosting drugs, vacuum pumps and by not worrying about it. Yes, worrying can make it worse; it's a vicious circle. The good news is that the medical profession can do much to help. Always ask your doctor for help here rather than be tempted by those spam emails offering you Viagra™ and other performance-enhancing drugs.

Boredom

If you've been making love to the same person for decades, you both might be getting bored with doing the same old stuff. The symptom you experience might simply be a lack of enthusiasm or desire; the underlying cause is that sex has become repetitive.

The good news about boredom is that it is easily rectified. You simply both need to recognize the problem and deal with it without embarrassment. It might be many years since you looked at pornography, but if you're looking for inspiration this might be a place to go. Looking with your partner will make it feel more wholesome!

There are also a lot more so-called 'adult shops' around now. These have moved from being sordid curtain-doored outlets in shady streets to high street stores. The internet also is a good place to shop for manuals, vibrators and other purchases that might put the spark back into your sex life.

A new partner

If you're recently divorced, separated or widowed after a long and happy relationship, starting again can be daunting. Many normally virile men find themselves hamstrung by impotence, embarrassment and fear when seeking to start a new sexual relationship.

Good communication is the key to overcoming this kind of sexual hurdle. Talking about it frankly and openly will make it easier to overcome. It will often also strengthen the relationship.

Sexually transmitted diseases

You may be surprised to learn that an increasing number of people over 50 are contracting sexually transmitted diseases. There are a number of reasons for this, not least that more older people are sleeping around.

If you've been in a long-term relationship it's easy to assume that so has everybody else. This is not the case and so if you find yourself in bed with someone new, don't be tempted to risk unprotected sex. It's fair to say that because fertility declines as menopause approaches, so the risk of pregnancy falls. However, this encourages more older people to make love without using condoms and so sexually transmitted diseases increase. Don't take unnecessary risks.

If indeed you do think you've contracted a sexually transmitted disease, getting treatment might not be as embarrassing as you think. Your own doctor will be professional and discrete, or there are specialist 'genito-urinary medicine' clinics where you can be treated anonymously.

Sex was never intended to be a competitive sport. You only have a problem with sex when you are no longer happy with your sex life. Enjoy!

Action plan: building a plan together

Life on your own can be pretty boring; we were designed to live with a partner. With people living longer these days, it's not unusual to see relationships last 60 years or longer. That certainly was not the case in earlier centuries when life expectancy was far shorter.

When you hit 50, you could be at any stage of a relationship. However, potentially you could be with your current partner for many decades to come. It makes good sense then to work at making your relationship better (and few are not capable of some improvement).

Here's an action plan for your relationship. It will enable you to put into action any or all of the topics covered in this chapter. Only you know if they're relevant to you. Don't deceive yourself!

1 **Make and compare lists.** Sit down with your partner and write down your answers to the following questions:
   a What do I like most about you?
   b What would I most like to change about you?
   c What's the best thing we've ever done together and why?
   d What single experience would I least like us to repeat?
   e If we spent more time together, what would I like to do?
   f What would make our sex life even better?

2 **Discuss any surprises.** Be careful not to be critical or subjective. Exploring the surprises will help you understand each other even better than you do now.

3 **Agree what's reasonable.** You might decide to change a few things to accommodate unfulfilled ambitions and new ideas. Set yourselves some goals and agree what it is reasonable to expect from each other. (Differing perceptions of what is reasonable is one of the largest causes of dissent in a relationship.)

4 **Experiment.** Try some of the suggestions in this chapter. Do more research around the areas you both want to work on. Even go shopping if you want to buy some bits and pieces to jazz up your sex life.

5 **Reflect and review.** This sounds awfully formal, but should not be so at all. You simply need to make time to look back, say once a month, to see how your relationship is growing.

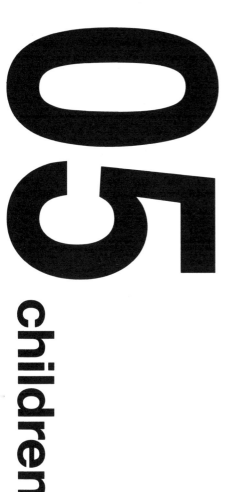

05

children

In this chapter you will learn:
- how to cope with adolescent children
- the implications of becoming a father at 50
- the benefits of being a grandfather.

Love them or hate them, children are part of everyone's life. In your 50s, you might have adult children, babies or grandchildren, or all three. On the other hand, you might not be a father, but inevitably those you know and care about will have children. You can't escape them, so here are some ways to cope with the challenges they pose.

How to have an adult relationship with your grown-up kids

Your children growing up will probably affect you in two ways. Firstly, you will be delighted that they are now less demanding on you. Secondly, you will suddenly feel old, as your house is now home to adults who are younger, fitter and facing longer futures than yourself. This is quite normal and you have to avoid your anxieties turning into resentment.

You have already been through your own young adulthood and hopefully have many happy memories of those times. Even if you do not, it is folly to encourage your children to act out your missed opportunities.

What they are going through

The years that follow adolescence are amongst the most eventful of our lives. It is easy to forget the sense of adventure we felt at this time. Although well past puberty and probably comfortable with their sexuality and desires, much else is changing for your kids.

University means combining the independence of living away from home, usually for the first time, with financial dependence on you. The excitement that comes with broadening horizons is tempered by the reality of financial insecurity.

Then, there is a career to consider. Long-harboured childhood ambitions can be dashed by one set of poor exam results. Realities and expectations collide and things never quite seem to be as they had expected.

Relationships are steadying down. From the early romances, longer running affairs develop with lots more pain when they end. However, as they become longer lasting, they lead to the challenges of setting up a new home.

Through all of these significant events parents are important. You will be a useful source of advice, often reluctantly sought, and necessary finance. It's a tough time for your kids and they need your support, not your interference.

What you're going through

Your son's razor left on the bathroom sink is a stark reminder that you are no longer this household's dominant male. If you both live with his mother, the chances are she devotes more of her time to meeting his needs than your own. You feel upstaged, overrun and beaten.

Couple this with someone buying you this book, a reminder that you're hitting 50, and it can get really depressing. In fact, depression is how many men respond to their relegation to second division in their own homes.

It suits the young adults to have Father kept in his place and Mother at their beck and call. For one thing, he poses a threat to their perceived adult independence. For another, he is a role model they would rather not be seen to emulate. However successful you are, your kids will not take kindly to be reminded of it. Their focus is on their own lives and you have done your job and are not needed for the time being.

Of course this will change later, or whenever a major crisis strikes. Fathers are good at sorting out problems, especially financial ones!

If you have daughters, you'll be well used to their manipulative ways as they flirt their way through their teens, learning 'mancraft' at your expense. Then there are those boyfriends, initially polite but once established quick to put you back in your place. It's not surprising that resentments grow, however loving the family, as your fledglings flap their wings and bruise you as they struggle to fly free of the nest.

Sometimes, your children will make life choices very different from your own. They may be gay, vegetarian or embrace religion with more fervour than you can muster. If this happens to you, remember that they are your children first, and anything else second. Your love for them should be unconditional.

Chris

When his daughter Anne started bringing boys home, Chris prided himself on being mature about it. He welcomed each young man into the family home, plied him with beer and tried hard not to lie awake at night wondering when they were going to come home.

One morning, a particularly persistent young man called Martin appeared at breakfast time. Chris almost choked on his toast as the full meaning of this new development dawned on him.

His partner had to point out to Chris that their daughter and Martin were the exact ages they had been when they'd first made love in the back seat of her old Morris. Chris had to think about this for a while, then accepted, to an extent, that his little girl really had turned into young woman.

Making rules

If you are not as liberal minded as Chris in the example above, you should make sure you set clear ground rules for what is acceptable in your house. If your attitudes are very different to those of your children, they will respect you more for upholding them than for letting your standards slip. Avoid making judgements, but don't hold back if you feel the need to impose rules.

Ways to cope

One answer lies in a psychological technique called 'transactional analysis'. This piece of jargon actually describes a pretty fundamental set of behaviours that will help you manage your children effectively. It's used a lot in relationship counselling and even sales training. This is because it enables you to change the way someone relates to you, by changing your style of approach to them. Here is a simple explanation:

There are three states:

Parent: authoritative, nurturing, dominant

Child: obedient, demanding, submissive

Adult: mature, responsible, equal

As a relationship needs two people, each will adopt one of the three styles.

Parent–child: the parent dominates and the child submits

Child–child: couples often play together and thus become child-child

Adult–adult: both are equal and treat each other as such

Your relationship with your children will have started, not surprisingly, as a parent–child one. You were always right because you were grown up and they were not. As they grew up, they pushed at this which inevitably leads to tension and perhaps even conflict. This is most noticeable when your children are adolescents.

Your challenge now that they are adult is to treat them as such. In return, they are more likely to treat you as an adult. It's largely to do with the phrases you use and the extent to which you try to dominate or subvert.

Here are some simple ways you can phrase conversations with your children to be adult–adult:

- ask their opinion rather than imposing your own
- share facts and seek discussion rather than dictating
- listen to what they have to say and mirror (repeat back) the words they use in your response
- soften your dialogue to avoid words such as 'must', 'should', 'will'. Instead use less harsh words, such as 'would', 'could', 'might'.
- value their expertise. At seven they were probably more adept than you with the video recorder; today their skills will exceed yours in many areas.
- beware of overplaying your trump card: experience. Sometimes it's better to let them find things out the hard way than to try and protect them from what you see as a risk.

The successes you achieve as your children move further into adulthood will make it easier for them to establish a stronger relationship with you when you are both older. Grandchildren are not something you want to think about, unless you already have some. The fact is that the birth of your children's children will open up a whole new world for you to discover together.

Look on their early adult years as your sabbatical from parenthood. When they produce babies, you want to be in a position to support them as well as enjoy the fun that being a grandparent can deliver.

Surviving becoming a father in mid-life

You only really know you're grown up when you become a father. When your first child is born you know you are a man because here in front of you is your newborn, dependent child. It also proves that your equipment is fully functioning and that's a confidence booster too!

When you have a child in mid-life, it is quite a different experience. For one thing you may already have had one family and seen them grow up. For another, you're older, wiser and better able to cope.

More daunting perhaps is the thought of attending your child's graduation ceremony in your early 70s. Or how about babysitting your grandchildren in your 80s? Plus the realization that you might not live long enough to see your offspring settled into their own middle years.

Becoming a parent in mid-life brings its own, rather special challenges and opportunities. If you are that man, or the idea of it is in your mind, here are some things you might like to consider. There is no right or wrong answer though; it's your life and quite different from anybody else's.

Helping your other children cope

If you have already had children, they may well be shocked that you've given them a new sibling. It will be more traumatic for them if their mother was not involved.

Of course your children know you have sex, otherwise they would not be here, but adult children rarely appreciate tangible evidence of your mid-life potency. When there are only a few years between children, it doesn't bother the kids when a new one pops up (apart from the usual sibling rivalries that is).

There are benefits of course, not least the ability to share the new child's upbringing with your older children. With encouragement, they can become almost like favourite uncles and aunts to the new arrival. The experience also helps them prepare for parenthood themselves. There are benefits!

If you encounter challenges when a new baby appears, here are some practical tips to help you cope:

- include them as much as you can so they feel involved
- reassure them that you still have time for them

- discuss money if they're worried about what might happen when you die
- recognize that if you have a new partner, your children's mother might also be fuelling their discomfort – give them opportunities to discuss their feelings with you.

Managing the money

In theory, you are more likely to be able to afford to raise a child in mid-life than when you are young. However, you may well need to look again at your retirement planning.

If your baby is born when you are 50, he or she will probably be at university when you are retired. This means you need to plan your finances to give you more cash at a time when you many no longer be earning. Equally important is the need to make sure you don't erode your reserves to fund education and then find yourself hard up in old age.

Consider saving more now to cover for those years when you might be funding students without earning a salary!

Health

Young children are great for your health and fitness! They can literally keep you young and will have you running around from dawn to dusk.

You need to look after your health and particularly be wary of the risk of injuring yourself; you might not be a supple as you once were! Having said that, beware of behaving old. Let your youngster persuade you to do more than you might otherwise attempt. Surprise yourself!

Image

School events and children's parties are where you may be most aware of your age. Being mistaken for a grandfather does little for your self-esteem. Your child will also be very aware that compared to his or her friends, you are an 'old parent'. This fact will be the source of much playground discussion, whether you like it or not.

Practical ways to deal with this could include:

- wearing a 'proud dad' T-shirt at school events
- introducing yourself as his/her father to spare people the embarrassment of getting it wrong

- getting fit so you can beat younger dads on Sport's Day

Things to perhaps avoid include:

- trying to be trendy and look younger than you are
- pretending to be granddad
- apologizing for your age (instead extol the benefits of late parenthood).

Becoming a parent late in life will probably do your image no end of good, as people, not surprisingly, associate fatherhood with sexual prowess. Some of your friends will both envy and admire your courage, whilst others will focus on the challenges you may face in the future as both you and your child grow older.

As with everything about life, there are both advantages and disadvantages to parenthood in mid-life. Make sure you take full advantage of the opportunities and enjoy the experience.

Becoming a grandparent

More than 90 per cent of parents become grandparents. It's a statistical fact that if you've got children, they'll likely as not have children too. If you're a man around 50 the arrival of your first grandchild serves as a stark reminder that you're no longer young.

The realization that your children are now responsible adults, in established relationships and starting families of their own can be a shock. An even bigger shock is the unplanned pregnancy resulting from your son or daughter's carelessness.

When the arrival of a grandchild is first announced, your first duty is to support your child. Just because your child is becoming a parent, doesn't mean they don't still need parenting themselves. In fact, in many ways, they need you more now because you have direct experience of what it is they are going through.

Dealing with the initial shock

Planned or not, the imminent arrival of your first grandchild can have a traumatic effect on you. You need to make time for yourself and be prepared for some roller-coaster emotions. You may be delighted, or dismayed, or even sometimes both.

If you do not approve, try not to let it show. It will help nobody and may drive a wedge between you and your child. Better to be non-judgemental and to focus on the practical issues. Your own experience will be invaluable to your child as he or she comes to terms with parenthood.

You will probably not feel that you are old enough to be a grandfather. All new grandfathers feel this way. Once you recover from the initial surprise, you have much that is exciting to look forward to.

What do grandfathers do?

It's unlikely that your own grandfathers are alive. If you're 50 they would have been born around 100 years ago. The world has changed an awful lot in that time.

There are, however, still some lessons you can learn from your own grandfathers, despite the fact that they may have been born when Queen Victoria was on the throne. Cast your mind back to your own childhood. What are your memories of your grandparents? Make a list of the most positive memories. These are the things you might want to be remembered for yourself in another 50 years' time.

If you ask children, they will tell you that the best grandfathers:

- take an interest in all that they do
- introduce them to new pastimes and interests
- listen to them when they want to get something off their chest
- give them treats that usually they are not allowed
- cheer the loudest when they win a race.

Benefits to you

Despite any initial reservations you may have, becoming a grandfather presents tremendous benefits to you. Some are obvious, others less so. Here are some really good things you can do when you become a grandparent:

- Enjoy their company and then give them back. It's rather like parenthood only without the responsibility.
- Reminisce about your own childhood. Grandchildren love hearing about what to them sounds like ancient history. Your children on the other hand, probably don't want to hear it all again.

- Loosen up. If middle age is starting to slow you down, keeping up with new youngsters will soon loosen you up. This applies to your mind as well as your body!

Your relationship with your child

The key message here is not to interfere. Your children have to raise their own children in whichever way they choose. Naturally you are concerned, but you need to step back and let them get on with it. This can be very difficult, although it's usually more of a problem for grandmothers than for you.

When your child becomes a parent, it does change your relationship with them. For one thing, you now have more in common and for another, you are also much more useful now. It's an opportunity to build a closer relationship with your child than perhaps you enjoyed since he or she was a child.

Many grandparents share childcare responsibility. This can enrich your relationship with your grandchildren, as well as give them an alternative to time with a childminder. Remember, though, that just as your grandchildren will benefit at times from spending time with other children at a nursery, so too will you need time to yourself. Why not suggest a mixture of professional childcare and time with you?

Golden rules for the new grandfather

1 Take an interest but don't interfere.
2 Don't spoil the child without first getting permission.
3 Listen to your grandchild, but don't take sides in family arguments.
4 Don't pry.
5 Make time for your grandchildren, however busy your life may be.

Why being young today is so different to being young in your day

When we were boys, things were very different. For one thing the world's population in 1960 was half what it is today, and there were ten million less people living in the UK. Around 70 per cent of men smoked; the average wage was less than £200 a year and only one in three families owned a car.

Today's youngsters take for granted things like the internet, mobile phones, central heating and indoor toilets. It's no wonder they look at you incredulously when you start telling them what life was like in the 1960s.

There are some things that were definitely better in our day. The UK homicide rate has more than doubled since 1960, suggesting that we live in a far more violent society now than then. People certainly felt safer then and children were allowed to play outdoors, unsupervised. The world was a very different place.

Ways they see the world differently

Young people, not surprisingly, see the world very differently to us. They often feel more confident, self-assured and in control of their destiny. They communicate with friends frequently and are as likely to use on-line chat or text to message as they are to pick up the phone.

That's not to say they don't also at times feel vulnerable. The cost of living is high, many start work with a sizeable student debt and buying a first home has probably not been so difficult for decades.

Here are some ways they may see the world differently to you:

- **Work–life balance.** Most young people put life before work. They will not sacrifice their leisure time for study or work in the way you might have done.
- **Ambition.** Today's young person does not believe in climbing the career ladder. They expect to make rapid progress when they start work and will quickly become frustrated if things take longer than they expect.
- **Frequent change.** Our generation were raised by parents who probably had a job for life. Most of our generation will see several changes during a career with today's young people seeing even more. You may have been at times reluctant to change. Today's youngsters welcome change.
- **New not used.** Today's young people are not used to repairing things, indeed little now is designed to be mended when it breaks. Today, everyone buys new.
- **Save the planet.** Young people today are incredibly environmentally aware. They are also far more socially conscious and much more likely than we were to make sacrifices for the common good. The green movement has been recognized by us all as being vital to our future. Young people take this far more seriously than we usually do.

How not to appear a dinosaur

Older people like to talk about the past. You know that already from the old people you know. What may not be so apparent is that young people might be saying the same about you.

Nostalgia is a wonderful comfort to us all. The trouble is that one man's nostalgia can be rather boring to a younger man. You or I might talk enthusiastically about *Muffin the Mule* or an Austin Cambridge. To the young the conversation only goes to prove the point that you're over the hill.

To avoid appearing a dinosaur to today's young people:

* keep yourself up-to-date with current affairs
* show an interest in things that interest them but are a mystery to you
* be positive about the future
* don't keep referring to the past
* act your age, not theirs!

How to bridge the gap

In short, you need to take young people seriously and respect their views and opinions. That way they will take you seriously too. As you can see, they may well have a quite different perspective on the world to you, but that's not to say that either of you is right, or wrong.

The techniques listed already in this chapter that will help you with your own children and grandchildren are equally effective with any young person. You need to acknowledge the differences between you without claiming that you are in any way superior.

Action plan: improving your relationships with young people

Before you actually set out to improve your relationships with the young people in your life, you need to understand your motives. It is quite natural and healthy for there to be a generation gap. It's how young people create their own individual and collective identity.

That said, they are deeply influenced by what older people say and do to them. Self-confidence can appear to be strong, but in reality it is easily damaged. Here's your five-step action plan to help you relate better to the young people you care about:

1 **Understand your goals.** What you are seeking has to be realistic and of value to both of you. Wanting to make your child, grandchild or the kids next door more respectful is not enough. Not, that is, unless you are prepared to earn their respect. Most of us want younger people to recognize that we have some value to them. Often we can easily see what's in it for us. To succeed, you need to be equally clear about the benefits to the young person.

2 **Communicate positively and consistently.** Avoid being judgemental or negative. Do not blow hot and cold, nor should you be critical of the young person or anything they may value. Cast your own mind back to when you were young. Did your father encourage you to listen to pop music or was he critical of it? Remember that in his day, Tchaikovsky was a 'pop composer', just as Lennon and McCartney were in ours. Tomorrow's fondly remembered icons from this decade are currently establishing their reputation. Don't assume you know better than people half your age.

3 **Listen and don't always try to understand.** Youth culture is meant to be mystifying to you and the rest of our generation. Pay attention, listen, but don't always pretend to appreciate value or even always understand. Young people will respect you all the more if you behave your age and don't pretend to really know your way around their world.

4 **Put yourself in their shoes.** Just as your parents and their generation frustrate you, so too do you frustrate the next generation down the chain. One of the delights of being 50 is that you can sit comfortably in the middle, annoying those younger whilst also being annoyed by those older. This should give you a tremendous insight into how you are regarded by the young. Usually, you have make a real effort to put yourself in their shoes and see yourself from their perspective. This is both enlightening and worthwhile.

5 **Don't expect too much.** We all lead busy lives. That applies to the young, the old and to you too. Whilst what each generation does may differ, it's all of equal importance. The media paints very glossy pictures of family life that in reality are experienced by very few people. As you settle into your role as a middle-aged man, you must not expect too much of young people. They will only have so much time to spare for you, however valuable your contribution to their lives.

06

parents

In this chapter you will learn:
- why your parents still worry about you
- how to manage their expectations of you
- ways to encourage them to lead fuller lives themselves.

We all had parents once. You might still have yours, as well as being perhaps a parent yourself. The interactions between the generations can be really positive. They can also become minefields, likely to blow up in your face if you make one false move. Here's how to handle parents, or any other senior people who might take a close interest in your well-being!

How to stop them worrying about you

Just as you may struggle to let go of your own children, so at the same time your own parents may be struggling to let go of you. It seems that however old you become, your parents always think of you in some ways as a child.

As your parents grow old, and if you're 50 they probably are growing old, their relationship with you will be gradually changing. Hopefully they are in good health and independent, in which case they present no real challenge to you. If however their health is beginning to fail, you will be witnessing the gradual change in relative position. Whereas once you were reliant on them, they will slowly become reliant on you.

That doesn't stop them worrying about you. In fact, ageing parents worry all the more, feeling perhaps that they are a burden to you and are in some ways holding you back.

Why parents find it hard to let go

However old you are, your parents will always be older. They'll have experienced the stage you're at now somewhere between 20 and 40 years ago. Therefore, whatever milestone you reach, they'll have reached it first.

The same probably applies to death. They will in all probability die before you do. This is not a nice subject to consider, but it is likely to be one that crosses your parents' minds daily. Your increasing maturity serves to remind them of their own mortality. It's not nice, but it's real.

Keeping you young, in a strange psychological way, keeps them young too. If they can chastise you, or guide you as they always have done, it helps them much more than it hinders you.

Your dilemma then is how much to allow your parents to interfere in your life for their own good. Whilst they may not accept or even recognize the motive, ageing parents can take too close an interest in your affairs.

Of course not all parents are ever like this. Some have a good grasp of their own lives and where they are at with them. They do not need to lean on you in this way for support.

If your parents are leaning on you, here are some tips to help you cope with the situation:

- **Tell them you love them.** They may be annoying, but they are your parents. You love them despite the fact that they can also drive you mad!
- **Share your good times.** Let them see how successful you are. Encourage them to compare your life achievements with their own. Take care not to say 'I've done better than you', because you've had more opportunities than they did. (Equally, if you have high achieving parents, don't be daunted; they should still be encouraged to value your successes.)
- **Tell them your ambitions.** You may not think they can help, but don't deny them the opportunity to try. Sometimes parents can help you see the obvious.
- **Seek their advice.** Find aspects of your life where their input will be welcomed and seek their advice. They probably want to feel they're helping; it doesn't really matter to them what they're helping you with.
- **Don't put them down.** Constantly reminding your parents that they are past it will not encourage them. Listen to what they want to say and be tactful when you respond.

New ideas for old parents

One positive way to stop your parents worrying about you is to give them something else to worry about. That's not to say you should introduce new problems to their lives. More that you should introduce them to new interests.

When people get old they tend to reduce their commitments rather than increase them. In other words, they give up more than they take up. This gives them lots of free time which they have to fill. Your challenge is to help them fill their time with new activities. There's no reason why anyone should not be taking up new interests and hobbies at any age. The only constraints are likely to be either physical, or simply a lack of inspiration!

It would not be good, for example, to introduce your mother to needlework if her eyesight is bad. Nor would bowls suit your father if he has trouble balancing! Spend a little time researching things they might try, then dare them to do it – it can certainly stop them worrying about you!

Managing their increasing vulnerability

Nobody likes getting old. In fact many choose to ignore the fact. As your parents grow old you will feel a growing sense of responsibility for them. You may also find that their gradual change into 'old people' acts as a disquieting reminder of what awaits you in the future.

How your parents might grow old

The signs are sometimes hard for them to notice, but may be painfully clear to you. Typical 'symptoms' of getting old include:

- becoming intolerant of late nights and change generally
- food fussiness and the avoidance of spicy dishes
- aches and pains that prompt complaint but are non-specific
- increasing deafness
- poor memory – they may tell you the same things repeatedly.

Plus of course they begin to look old. What's more you become increasingly aware that it's been years since they bought anything new for their home and everything is beginning to look run down and tired.

Again this is not true of all old people. Some old women remain incredibly fashion and image conscious well into old age. Some men are still putting a full week in at the office in their 80s. Everyone is different.

Keeping them 'young'

If your parents become unable to care for themselves (and this happens to surprisingly few people) you are faced with some tough decisions. Selling up and moving them in with you, or into sheltered accommodation, is a minefield you want to steer clear of if possible.

Here are some good ways you can keep your parents independent for as long as possible. They may need your encouragement and support, but in the long term, it's important for you all that you keep them 'young'.

Organizations such as Help the Aged (UK) can provide helpful information on what help and benefits might be available to your parents as their need for support increases. Their doctor can also usually advise them on these matters.

Eat well

It's tempting to make life simple and eat convenience foods. This is a particular challenge for men living on their own after a lifetime of being cooked for by mother then wife. Good diet is vital for good health. Poor diet can reduce resistance to illness and also cause unwanted weight gain. To help them eat well:

- stock their larder with things that are good for them
- buy a simple cookbook and gadgets for the 'home alone' father
- cut out and send them recipes you find
- don't nag them!

Exercise

I've seen old men put their walking stick to one side and clamber onto the exercise bike at the gym. They may not peddle fast, but they are keeping fit. Exercise does not come easily to older people, yet it can deliver huge benefits. A good exercise programme can improve mobility, strengthen bones, keep away coughs and colds and reduce the likelihood of depression. To help them exercise regularly:

- buy them membership of the local gym (choose one that specializes in older people)
- buy them a dog so that they at least take long walks
- encourage them to go on a sponsored cycle ride
- buy them swimming lessons.

Kick habits

In the 1960s, 70 per cent of men and 40 per cent of women smoked. It could be that your parents have smoked for 40 or even 50 years. It's not too late to encourage them to give up. Even after decades of abuse, lungs and hearts improve when you give up. In fact, why not have a heart to heart with your parents about their lifestyle and how they might live more healthily. Be realistic and seek moderation rather than abstinence! To help them kick bad habits:

- treat them to help with an addiction (perhaps hypnotherapy)
- set a good example and give up yourself!

- help them to set goals and celebrate with them when they succeed
- introduce replacement activities that are more healthy.

It's also good to encourage your parents to recognize that looking after their body will keep it working for longer. Perhaps you might even encourage them to visit their doctor for an annual MOT!

When age takes its toll

Inevitably there will come a time when your parents find themselves unable to cope as well as they once did. What they need from you at this point is understanding, compassion and encouragement. The encouragement is especially important as they might be tempted to give up.

When you get older and things start to fail, the best way forward is to focus on getting the most mileage out of what is left. Once older people start to assume that things will deteriorate, they will.

Common pitfalls and how to avoid them

For generations, ageing parents have presented problems to their adult children. If you are worried about what the future holds for you, at least you know you're not the first person to experience it.

There are a number of common pitfalls into which people like you or me often fall. It can be tough trying to balance your own needs against your understandable sense of commitment to your parents.

Not enough money

Parents rarely want to admit to being hard up. The fact is though, that old age can be financially a very difficult time. Not all pensions keep pace with inflation and unexpected bills can cause problems.

Sometimes older people make decisions about money with the wrong objectives in mind. Many feel the need to do without the things they need to preserve what they see as your inheritance.

However embarrassing it may be for you both, it is always wise to discuss money openly with your parents. They need to understand how important their legacy is to your future. Some people rely on inheritance to fund their own old age. Others quite frankly don't need the money and encourage their parents to spend it.

There are a number of options open to older people who may be 'asset rich and cash poor'. The best known of these is equity release. This is in effect a mortgage. There are various kinds of arrangement and some are better than others.

If your parents are facing money problems, consider:

- introducing them to an independent financial adviser you trust
- encouraging them to find out exactly what they have got (it's not uncommon for investments to be forgotten!)
- helping them prepare a simple household budget and see if savings can be made.

Health 'secrets'

Parents like to protect their children from upset. They don't want to worry you, so keep secret from you any health problems that occur. At worst, they may conceal the diagnosis of a terminal illness and push you away so that you are less likely to spot the symptoms. Less severe but no less distressing are the depressing array of debilitating conditions that can beset the aged. Too embarrassed to tell you, they keep it secret and you are denied the opportunity to do much to help.

This seeming rejection can hurt, particularly if you find out the cause when it's too late to spend as much time with a seriously ill parent as you might have liked. You can help avoid this pitfall by:

- being open as a family and discussing health in a matter of fact way
- making sure they know you would never see their troubles as a burden
- asking direct questions if you suspect something's not right
- not panicking if they share bad news.

Over downsizing

When older people begin to notice that age is starting to bite, they often decide to downsize. This can be a good thing to do, particularly if a bungalow by the sea has long been a lifelong retirement ambition.

However, sometimes in their enthusiasm to 'be ready for old age' people make too many changes too quickly. A smaller home, perhaps without stairs is a wise move, but combining this with the challenge of moving to a new part of the country can be overwhelming.

Sometimes people downsize then wish they hadn't. It can be very difficult to upsize, so here are some questions to put to your parents before they commit to anything too drastic!

- Planning for old age and infirmity is sensible, but how many years do they think it'll be before they are infirm? (It might be ten years!)
- They may still love gardening – do they think they will be happy next summer in a seafront apartment?
- Would they like you to help find somewhere?
- Do they think it's too soon after 'X' to be making big decisions?

Sometimes, of course, you only find out about the pitfall when your parents have fallen in it. If this happens, be sympathetic and try to help them climb out. Saying 'I told you so' helps nobody.

Opportunities you might not have considered

It's sometimes quite easy to see what everyone else is doing. It is harder to find something different to do yourself. As your parents age they will increasingly be led by what they see others of their age do. Confidence may slip in later life and there's a tremendous comfort in following the example of friends and acquaintances.

You might consider encouraging your parents to think outside the proverbial box. Here are some useful starting points.

Park homes

Park homes are factory built bungalows. They are supplied ready furnished and sited on exclusive parks, developed entirely with this kind of housing. Because they are of non-standard (bricks and mortar) construction, they are cheaper than conventional bungalows of the same size. Being fully furnished, they provide a fresh start, free of the clutter built up over a lifetime.

Most of the parks developed with these homes only sell to people aged over 50. In reality, most residents are retired and this creates a very pleasing environment, free of the bustle of modern life. Additionally, security is good, as many parks are gated with security passes for residents.

Park homes enable older people to:

- release equity and not sacrifice comfort or convenience
- join a thriving community of like-minded, similarly aged people
- live in a secure, quiet environment.

Steve

A successful solicitor, Steve was proud that he had left his working class background behind and enjoyed material success. His own children went to private school and everything was fine.

Except, that is, his parents. Now in their 70s, they had never been well off and, although they owned their home, living from month to month was a challenge.

Then a client of his, who owned a development of park homes, showed Steve some new homes he had placed in a particularly leafy setting on the edge of the park. The penny dropped; his parents could sell up, move here and bank a sizeable sum to provide for all the things they could no longer afford.

Initially reluctant, the old couple eventually saw the logic. One year after the move they say they would never go back. They love the sense of community and have made lots of new friends.

Buy the place next door

If your parents want to be closer to you, but you can see the drawbacks of them living with you, why not both sell and buy neighbouring properties? You can then be close enough to keep an eye on them, yet you both have your own front doors you can close when you want some privacy.

There are many options when you start to think about pooling resources and buying something that suits you both. Having your parents next door also has its benefits, for example:

- you can look after each others' homes and pets during holidays
- visiting no longer requires a long journey
- things can be easily shared
- if you eventually inherit their place, you have an easy to manage asset to rent out.

Emigrating

People emigrate at all ages. Why not encourage your parents to buy a place in the sun? They may benefit from a kinder climate free of those cold, damp winters. Pensions and medical care are similar throughout the EU and the cost of living can actually be lower.

If you feel you see too much of them, encouraging them to live abroad will make visiting both less frequent and more enjoyable.

Adopt a granny

It might be that you no longer have your parents. There are plenty of older people around who have no children too. Life can get pretty lonely when you're old and alone.

If you have a family, it can be rewarding for all concerned to 'adopt' an old person or old couple. Of course this is not a formal arrangement, but perhaps you have a near neighbour who would welcome being 'adopted'?

Benefits of 'adopting a granny' include:

- they feel part of a family again and can take an interest in life
- your children learn about older people and enjoy that 'grandparent' experience they are currently missing
- they have someone willing to help out when there's a problem
- you have someone older taking an interest in you.

Home care

There is a trend away from residential care for the elderly. It is expensive, potentially disruptive and takes the old person away from all that is familiar to them.

When people become too frail to cope with day-to-day life, it's possible to arrange for them to receive the care and support they need in their home. It's no longer assumed that they will simply sell up and move into an old folks' home (as their own parents may well have done).

Benefits of care in the home include:

- support can be arranged as it is needed, rather than 'all or nothing'
- independence is retained, as is self-respect and dignity
- they live in a familiar environment and don't lose touch with friends
- it costs less than residential care.

If you are facing challenges with your parents, do seek out innovative solutions. You don't have to accept the obvious answers.

Action plan: your list of things to discuss with your parents

Discussing your parents' life challenges is the reverse of what you are probably accustomed to. However much you are able to build an adult relationship with them, you will remain, deep down in their minds, their child.

It is a fact that we start our lives as children and in many ways end them the same way. As people age they inevitably retreat from the confusion that is everyday life and take pleasure from simpler, more familiar things. This helps them cope, but also increases their vulnerability.

You face a number of challenges when it comes to being what your parents might term a 'good son'. Your own life is probably pretty full and you're also dealing with this thing called mid-life. You have to balance bolstering their self-esteem with your natural desire to finally shrug off their 'helping hands'. Here to help you bring together all that is in this section, is a ten-point list of positive things to do with your ageing parents:

1 **Let them be parents.** Involve them in aspects of your life where their input is welcome. This makes them feel wanted and valued. It also makes them less likely to interfere in the things you consider to be none of their business. Parents worry about their children and want to help. Give them things to help with and they will feel that this role is being fulfilled. Shut them out and they may try to intrude.

2 **Give them 'permission' to be old.** They may not like getting old and feel embarrassed by their declining abilities. Make

allowances for them and don't make a big deal of it. Encourage them to try new things you know will be within their ability. Compensate for the things they may find difficult. The gadgets we all joke about when we're 50 – stairlifts and bath-hoists – become annoyingly necessary for many old people seeking to retain their independence. They'll be more likely to invest in these gadgets if you introduce the idea gently and without humour!

3 **Don't let them give up.** There are three decades between 70 and 100. You can be old for a very long time. It's possible to take up new interests, start new organizations and much, much more when you're old. It's never too late to start something new. Your opportunity is to introduce new ideas and encourage them to experiment. It is true to say that when you stop anything late in life, it's much harder to start again.

4 **Keep them healthy.** Likely as not, your parents were children during the Second World War. Food was rationed and central heating rare. Diet and health were very different in their day. Now that food is cheap and plentiful, their home is warm and comfortable, life is very different. Encourage them to eat healthily and cut down on any harmful habits. Keep them physically active too.

5 **Be frank and open with them.** Encourage your parents to discuss those things you've perhaps never discussed with them before. Their finances, their fears, what they want to happen should they become incapable of making decisions for themselves. It may help if you let them into aspects of your life you've not shared before. Get to know your parents as well as they know themselves.

6 **Discourage them from springing surprises.** They may want to downsize, emigrate or sell up and join a commune. Whatever their plans or aspirations, you want them to feel you have the time and interest to discuss life options with them. Make them feel welcome when they call or visit. Avoid being presented with a *fait accompli.*

7 **Build bridges.** The points above assume you get on with your parents. It might be that, for whatever reason, you are estranged from them. Perhaps they disapproved of a life decision you once made and you've lost touch with them since. Sometimes quite trivial things, a teenage tattoo for example, can start the rift that never heals. However much they've hurt you in the past, give them a chance to make amends as they become older. You'll probably find that they've matured and so have you!

8 **Write it down.** Old people do strange things. If they keep their life savings in a cardboard box in the loft you need to know this. Otherwise when they die the next owner of their home could get a nice surprise when they have to repair the ball-cock in the roof! You need to have the contact details for their neighbours, or friends over the road who hold a spare key. Make sure that those who live and keep an eye on your parents also have your contact details. You never know when this might be important.

9 **Tell their story.** Every life is interesting, although too many are taken for granted. Your parents' memories and experiences will help you understand much about yourself. If you have children, they too will find their grandparents' stories fascinating. Sometimes old people find it difficult not to talk about the past, but why not add some structure and ask them to describe a different stage of their life each time you meet? They might even write it down. If they have old photographs, have them write on the back who the people are and where and when the picture was taken.

10 **Explore their faith.** There is no doubt that life is eventually followed by death. Understandably, many old people find this prospect daunting and often seek solace from their faith. Faith in its broadest sense is a topic to raise with them from time to time. Remember that having no faith is in many ways a faith in itself. Everyone believes something!

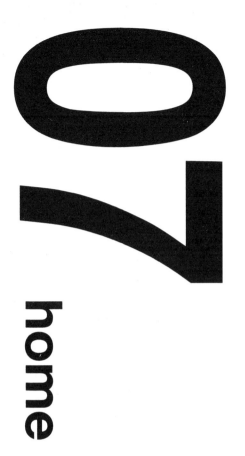

07

home

In this chapter you will learn:
- ways to decide if downsizing is for you
- easy ways to tackle home improvement challenges
- how to refresh your home.

They say that a man's home is his castle. You've probably worked your way up, and perhaps down, the housing ladder over the past quarter of a century. Your home, like your life, needs to constantly evolve to meet your needs and the needs of those you share this space with.

Opportunities presented by the 'empty nest'

If you accept that most men become parents in their late 20s, then it stands to reason that at 50, their children are at an age where they start leaving home. Many will say this is a more traumatic event for a mother, because she will feel in many ways that her work is done.

Coping with a house free of children for the first time in perhaps more than 20 years can be a real challenge. Coping with a partner who no longer needs to spend her life looking after children can be an even greater challenge. Alternatively, if your partner is not their mother, you may now be about to live alone together for the first time since you met.

Times have changed and your children are more likely perhaps than you were, to return to the family home should a job or relationship not work out. Your home may remain their refuge for many years to come. That too can inhibit your plans to radically change your life.

Setting them free

It is in most children's best interests to leave home. We have all met those middle-aged men who stayed at home and never married. They rarely seem to have a fulfilling life and are often painfully inhibited and shy. However much it might hurt you, your children need to fly the nest when they are ready.

For many, university is their first real taste of freedom. You have to accept that they'll make mistakes, eat badly, drink too much and if they've not done so already, discover sex. The good news is that universities know this and have lots of support in place should the student encounter problems.

Here are some ways you can help make this transition easier, without being seen to interfere:

- Leave them at home to fend for themselves now and again. It's good practice for the self-sufficient life they're about to lead.
- Make sure they know you'll always help; also that you won't be judgemental if they present you with problems that might shock.
- Get them used to budgeting and handling money responsibly.
- Convert their rooms into 'spare rooms' rather than leave them as teenage dens. Grasp the 'sex' nettle and buy double beds, for when they return with a partner.

Back to the beginning

If you are in a long-term relationship, the departure of the children puts you almost back at the beginning. There are less distracting chores to do, no other people to inhibit your conversation or activity and more choice than you've perhaps had since the early days of your relationship.

Just as one chapter in your life has closed, so is another, longer one opening. Of course you want your children to visit and inevitably they will, but you also have a chance to develop your life in new and interesting ways.

Here are some things you can discuss with your partner as you plan your new life as a couple, rather than as a family:

- What's going to change and how will we cope with it?
- What do we want to achieve over the next ten or so years?
- What are the things we've been putting off that we can now afford to do?

Emotional stuff

The departure of children from the family home prompts mixed emotions. On the one hand you are delighted they're starting independent life as adults. On the other you feel rejected and no longer needed. These roller-coaster feelings can put pressure on your relationship. In fact it could be that underlying problems surface at this time, because quite simply they have the opportunity to do so.

As with any emotional transition in your life, it's best not to rush in any one direction. Take your time and talk through any issues you may have. Remember that you will both view the departure of the children differently and that's OK.

If your relationship starts to creak, it might be worthwhile looking into counselling. Relationship counselling can take the heat out of conflict and improve communication between you and your partner. It is not unusual for relationship problems to emerge when the children are no longer around to distract you from each other.

New things to try

Above all else, you want to try new things, otherwise when the children leave home it can suddenly seem very quiet. Many parents say that they feel older and that in itself can be depressing. Here then are some things you can try that were not so easy before:

- make love on the sofa
- stay in bed until lunchtime
- take up a new hobby or sport
- have friends round more often.

When your children leave home, they are at the start of a new era in their lives. Make sure that it is also the start of a new era for you!

To downsize or not? An objective look at the options

Downsizing for you is a very different matter to downsizing for your parents. For them, it's probably about making life easier and often, freeing up equity. For you it's more likely to be about changing your life, not simply making it easier.

At 50 you are at an exciting stage in your life. Your children may have left home and money is probably not as tight as it was a few years ago. You might even be starting to feel comfortable. Your home though is your largest asset and one way you can make dramatic changes to your life, is to make dramatic changes to your home!

Why downsize?

At 50 you may be past the most expensive years of your life. You probably own a sizeable proportion of your home. You may also be tired of your current job and want to do something quite different whilst there is still time. If you've worked for the same firm for a long time, you might even be able to retire, or at least stop work and draw some income from your pension.

Reasons you might want to downsize include:

- to clear your mortgage and reduce your monthly bills
- to move to a new area that appeals to you
- to buy two smaller homes in different parts of the world
- to release equity to invest in a business venture or buy-to-let property portfolio.

You might also downsize to fund separation or divorce. That's not so positive a reason, but needs to be acknowledged all the same.

Alternatives to downsizing

If your motives for downsizing are purely to release capital to fund travel or a business venture, then there are alternatives. For example:

- You can borrow money against the equity in your property. If it's for business purposes, you will probably be able to allow the interest you pay against tax.
- You might actually start your business at home, using the space you have there rather than selling it to fund an office elsewhere.
- If you have spare rooms, why not rent them out and use the income?

Upsizing – the third option

Downsizing may be fashionable but upsizing can also be smart. It all depends what you want to achieve. Some people decide to run a bed and breakfast business, small shop or garden centre. These inevitably mean trading your home in for something larger. Upsizing can give you both a new home and a new career.

If your home is old, it may also need regular expensive maintenance. Your energy bills might also be high if it was built before the world became energy conscious. This gives you another opportunity to upsize.

Building your own home, either from scratch, using a timber frame kit, or converting a derelict property can give you more home for your money than if you bought something ready to live in.

Inevitably it means selling your existing home to free up the cash to build your new one. This involves hiring a mobile home and living on a building site for a few months. If you are good with your hands, you would even do some of the building work yourself.

Amazing downsizing case studies

To encourage you to consider some quite unusual lifestyle options, here are some examples:

- **Jon** sold his house at 50, trained as a Church of England priest and now works in London where he lives in a vicarage next to his church. He invested the proceeds from his house sale in two houses in the coastal resort where he plans to retire. Both are let and give him additional income.
- **Shaz** and his wife sold their home in Birmingham when he was 48. They bought a corner shop and takeaway business with the money and now live above the shop. Shaz was able to give up his job as a quality manager to start his own business.
- **Peter** is an artist. He sold his home when he was 55 and took early retirement. He now lives and paints on a canal boat in France. He sells his paintings to visiting tourists from the canal-side and has some cash invested to fall back on should times get hard.

How to refresh your home and your life

You might be very happy with your home. Some people buy a house when they marry, raise their children there and remain there for the rest of their lives. There is a wonderful sense of belonging that can evolve when you live somewhere for many years. Everything falls comfortably to hand and every nook and cranny conceals a memory.

Of course, if you have lived in the same place for 20 years or so, and that's quite possible, your home might also be looking a little tired! However, if you have moved a few times but taken everything with you, your home could still be in need of a makeover.

Improving your home, particularly in mid-life when your interests are changing and the children have gone, can be great fun. Don't simply see this as a chance to buy a new sofa, curtains and some pots of paint. Think more about how you can adapt your home to meet your needs for the second half of your life.

Food for thought

Do you or your partner love cooking and entertaining? If so, why not consider investing in a new, larger kitchen? If your kitchen is at the back of your house, you could extend out into a dining conservatory. Or if the children have left home and had their own sitting room downstairs, have the wall removed and add the space to a room you will use a lot.

Often, people buy a family home with lots of rooms. This is great when you have small children and want to be able to shut the door on toys and clutter. Why leave the room empty, or worse still, fill it with stuff, when the space could be used?

To make the best possible use of the space in your home, think about:

• exactly how many rooms you want and what they are to be used for
• how much you want to integrate house and garden
• your current interests and also your likely future needs.

Then measure your rooms, or if you have them, use the plans of your home to work out what you want and what you think is possible. If you can afford it, consult an architect who specializes in house conversions. You'll be surprised at how a good architect can suggest changes that are both cheaper and more effective than you would have thought of yourself. They can also advise on things like lighting, heating and drains.

Even if you can't afford to change your house round a lot, it's often worth starting with the ultimate 'if money was no object' plan. Almost inevitably this long-term vision will change the things you might choose to do right now.

Finding the cash

If you hate gardening and have a large plot, have you tried to sell part of it to someone wanting to build a house? Building plots can be squeezed into all kinds of spaces. Talk to your local planners to see if this is possible.

A more conventional way of funding a home makeover is to increase the mortgage. Sometimes changing to a new lender will give you more flexibility. Although it's tempting, try not to extend the term of your loan beyond its current limit. Remember though that if you have a pension plan, this will probably give you a cash lump sum when you decide to retire. See how much this might be. It's possible that you will be able to pay off the cost of your home makeover sooner than you thought.

Buying better

One advantage of maturity is that you are more experienced at spending money. You are also probably more discerning and look for quality more than perhaps you once did. This means you are more likely to make your money go further should you decide to buy new furniture, or perhaps the equipment you want to install for a new hobby.

New should not always mean brand new, but simply that something is new to you. You don't want to make your house look like a showroom, and you'll also appreciate that things do not remain new for long. Check out local auction rooms and sales, as well as second-hand dealers to find the pieces you want that will still look good in 20 years' time. Making over your home now might seem costly, but doing it again when you're in your 70s may, when the time comes, prove to be impossible.

As you celebrate mid-life with a home makeover, however bold or modest, do recognize that what you buy now, should and hopefully will last you for a very long time.

Getting things done

There are two kinds of men in the world. Those that love DIY and those that loathe it; there is no middle ground. If you are one of those who enjoys getting things done, are expert at repairing the washing machine and enjoy putting up shelves, then you can skip this section.

If on the other hand you really do wish you could avoid those white knuckle moments when you climb a ladder or push a power drill into the wall, this section should help you overcome the challenges of getting things done.

European legislation provides an easy excuse for those wishing to steer clear of electrical jobs more onerous than changing a light switch. Because of the dangers to you and your property, electrical, gas and some other work has to be done by a qualified specialist. You risk invalidating your home insurance if you dabble with danger and burn your house down as a consequence.

DIY

We all have to do some DIY jobs. Few tradesmen would want to come round to put up a picture or shelf. Yet even these simple tasks can turn into major challenges. Have you ever drilled through a cable in the wall and been plunged into darkness when the power trips out?

As your children set up their own homes you will want to demonstrate your value by helping them out. This desire to prove they need you encourages many DIY novices to give it a try. A further problem is that your children can rarely afford to pay someone to do the work, so it's down to you or your pocket!

There are three secrets to DIY. They are:

1 **Be confident.** Work out what you're going to deal with before you start. There are some excellent books and websites on DIY, although do print out website material just in case!
2 **Be prepared.** Apart from skill, the other advantage tradesmen have is that they invest in the right tools for the job. Improvization is one of the major causes of DIY disasters. Buying yourself some good tools, or hiring in the tackle you need, will give you a fighting chance of success. Particularly useful are those devices that detect pipes and wires in a wall. They really do save lives!
3 **Be patient.** DIY always takes twice as long as you expect. What's more, if you rush a job, you are much more likely to take even longer. There is no substitute for taking things apart slowly, writing down which wire went in which hole and having somewhere to put those tiny screws that so easily get lost.

Follow these three golden rules and you might even find yourself enjoying DIY. However, you also need to know your limits and avoid taking on more than you can handle. Without the confidence, skills or right tools, DIY can be dangerous!

Finding tradesmen

It seems that the bigger the firm, the bigger the bill. If you've called out one of those franchised drain jetting firms on a Sunday afternoon, you'll know that rapid response comes at a price.

The chances are though, that within a mile of your house lives a plumber who is an expert at unblocking drains, works for himself and charges around half the price. Of course there are exceptions that prove the rule, but in general, you'll get a better deal from the jobbing local tradesman than from his corporate counterpart, particularly if the job is relatively small.

As with DIY there are three golden rules that will help you find a good tradesman and avoid the sharks.

1 **Ask your neighbours.** Who have they used and who are they happy with? If someone gives good service, they are always happy to recommend them to others. If on the other hand they were ripped off, they won't tell you about it, let alone recommend the person who did it.

2 **Look for the vans.** Most tradesmen have a sign-written van. Look out for them around your neighbourhood. Note their details and don't be afraid to knock on the door to ask if the householder is pleased with their work. A clean van doesn't always mean a good worker, nor does a dirty van suggest someone to avoid.

3 **Find someone new.** It's a feature of the building world that good people serve their apprenticeship, learn the trade, then set up on their own. You can sometimes find newly established businesses by reading your local newspaper. You can also ask the organizations that advise start-ups to recommend one of their recent clients. Look up the Prince's Trust or your local Enterprise Agency.

There are only two ways to get things done. Do it yourself or pay someone else. For most of us, particularly those with a live-in partner, the third option, putting it off, is no option at all.

Second homes

Much of the focus of this chapter has been on downsizing and making more of what you have. It is also possible that you want to expand your property portfolio beyond simply owning the family home. Here are some options you might consider:

Holiday home

Holiday homes come in all shapes and sizes. From caravans by the sea that you visit every weekend to serviced city apartments that you let by the night. Holiday homes can give you much pleasure as well as the potential to earn an additional income.

If you plan to let your holiday home, it's usually better to use an agency than to try and do it yourself. Agencies cost money, but tend to deliver higher occupancy levels and so a greater overall return.

Buy-to-let

There are plenty of people who have made substantial sums from buy-to-let. This is where you buy houses and flats and then let them to generate sufficient income to repay any mortgage taken out when you buy the property.

As a general rule of thum you can borrow 85 per cent of the value of the place(s) you buy. It's also considered best to assume that your rental income will do no more than cover mortgage repayments, agency fees and maintenance. Your own return comes when you eventually either clear the mortgage or sell the property.

Buying abroad

Properties are often considerably cheaper abroad. This is particularly true of Eastern Europe and countries like Turkey and Greece. House prices can be inflated by a convenient local 'low cost' airline service from the UK. Equally, when an air route is withdrawn, property values can fall.

The law relating to property is often different in other countries. You need to check this out before committing yourself.

Many people also buy time-share properties abroad. If run by reputable companies, these can provide a unique opportunity to holiday overseas. Beware though of the timeshare touts who frequent many popular resorts.

Action plan: turn your house into a new home

In mid-life, your home becomes far more important to you. For one reason you probably spend more evenings in than you once did. And another is that you will by now have acquired lots of things. When you're young, home is simply somewhere to sleep and hang your shirts. At 50, it is far more important.

You also have probably shared your home for a good part of the last 20 years. Partners, children, perhaps even brothers, sisters and friends have occupied the space you call home.

Here then is a five-point action plan for your home.

1 **Whose home is it?** You know who lives with you now, but what about the future? Who is likely to arrive and who is likely to leave? Each person wants to have their own space which they can feel is theirs. Children put their mark on their bedrooms, often literally! Women tend to take control of the kitchen, however much that might not be politically correct. So where is your space? Define the parts of your home you can truly make your own.

2 **What do I want to change?** Your life has evolved over the years and you'll have acquired more clutter than you've disposed of; that's human nature. Work out what you want from your home and identify what's in the way of that happening. You might want to change, downsize, upsize or move to another part of the world. Match your plans for your home to any plans you are making for the rest of your life.

3 **Use your imagination.** Some people find it easier to visualize the possible than others. Look beyond the obvious and, if necessary, pay an architect to advise you how best you can re-configure rooms to meet your current needs. Look at other people's homes and be creative. Remember that the changes you make now might need to last a long time. For many people, the place they live in at 50 is the place they stay for the rest of their lives.

4 **Fund your dream.** Consider re-mortgaging to give you tomorrow's dream home today. Work out what money might be coming to you in a few years' time, for example from your pension, and factor that into your financial plan. You are probably better off than you realize.

5 **Do it and enjoy it.** Draw up a schedule for the work you want to do. Some you might enjoy doing yourself, other tasks you might hire someone to do for you. Take your time so that you can take pleasure from each step. If you try to rush it will become a chore. Finally, be sure to celebrate when you have finished.

One last thought: money invested in making your home a place you want to be, gives a better return than money you spend on going out.

08

money

In this chapter you will learn:

- some top money management tips
- how to make your money go further
- why other people are often not as well off as you might think.

Money lubricates life. Too little and life can be miserable, and you can never have too much. It is said that the over 50s are the wealthiest people in society. They have less debt, more savings and, apart from men who have become fathers in middle age, are over the most expensive stage of child-rearing.

Whether or not you identify with this, you will be interested in money. You'll want to know that any you have is working hard for you and any you owe is on competitive terms. The financial services industry has seen something of a revolution over the past ten years. Innovative new products and more aggressive marketing can make shopping around worthwhile.

Our parents' generation had a very different attitude to money. They saved rather than borrowed and remained loyal to one bank and one insurance company for life. There was perhaps less to choose between them and because customers were reluctant to swap providers, there was little incentive for the banks to innovate.

Money myths

Inevitably we picked up some of our parents' caution about money. Even if you ignore the advice they probably gave you as a boy, there may remain some money myths that need to be dashed. It's possible you've been just too busy of late to look properly at money matters. Here are some popular money myths:

Borrowing is bad

My father bought me a piggy bank and insisted I save half my pocket money. You too might have been told that saving is good and borrowing is bad. Of course if you borrow money to squander then yes, debt is bad. However, if you borrow money to buy your home, set up a business or simply spread the cost of something that will give you lasting pleasure, then surely borrowing is fine? The key point about borrowed money is that it is not yours. The sobering fact is that one day you will have to give it back.

If you're planning to borrow money, or maybe you have debts at high interest rates, here are some top tips on managing debt.

- Loans secured against property are usually the cheapest, whereas credit card debt is often the most expensive.

- The longer the term of the loan the more you'll pay. This is obvious when you think about it, but many people don't seem to realize it.
- Check for early payment penalties; you want the flexibility to pay off when it suits you, without penalty.
- If you're experiencing problems repaying debts, take professional advice. Remember that companies advertising their ability to deal with your debt have to earn their fees from someone – it might be you.

All saving is good

People used to save up to buy the things they wanted. They also used to save for a 'rainy day'. The consensus amongst advisers seems to be that you need three months' income tucked away somewhere safe. Beyond that, saving is really called investment.

Only rich people have investments

This is not strictly true. The financial services world is awash with investment products than enable you pool your money with that of others. You only have to open the Sunday papers to see a myriad of investment opportunities. Many require only modest initial investment. It's true that wealthy people have stockbrokers who advise them. They often invest in single shares and so need more specific advice.

The key difference between savings and investments is this:

- savings are where your capital is 100 per cent safe and earns you interest
- investments are where there is some risk and your capital grows as well as usually earning you a return on investment.

If you are considering investing money, you need to bear in mind:

- The extent to which you're prepared to risk losing money. Usually, the opportunity to gain high returns is matched by a high risk of losing some or all of your money.
- Unless you know what you are doing always take professional advice.
- There's nothing wrong with getting a second opinion. Getting five opinions though will confuse you.
- If a friend invites you to invest in their business think very, very carefully. There is a saying amongst professional

business investors that the first place the entrepreneur looks for money is to 'family, friends and fools'. Make sure you're not being a fool.

• No one can accurately predict the future.

If you have money to invest, consider:

• consulting an IFA to see what they recommend
• talking with your bank, who will have an investment specialist
• using a stockbroker (you can find them in local directories).

Always talk to several different advisers and only invest when you are sure you're making the best possible choice. Do not let any adviser push you into a decision you're not totally at ease with.

It is possible to get rich quick

When you're having one of those particularly 'middle-aged' gloomy days, getting rich quick can seem like the answer to all of your problems. However, there is no easy way to get rich quickly. Money will only come your way if you:

• **earn it** either as an employee or by setting up your own business
• **marry it** by getting hitched to someone with lots of money
• **inherit it** from someone who dotes on you, is very old and dies
• **steal it** in which case you'll probably go to prison and not need money anyway.

There are always things out there to trap the unwary. At your age, it is perhaps less likely you'll be caught by one, but they can appear really tempting. More dangerous is that sometimes people you know and respect become enmeshed in 'get rich quick schemes'. Often their only way out is to enmesh you too! Here are some things to be cautious of:

Pyramid schemes
You send money to a number of people and persuade others to join the scheme by doing the same. The organizers tell you that in time, all of the new joiners will be sending money to you. These schemes are illegal and rarely work.

Multi-level marketing (MLM)
Millions of people around the world earn a second income through joining an MLM business. There are many examples of

success and many examples where expectations were not met. If you are invited to join a network make sure that:

- you are realistic in what you expect
- you have the time to devote to the business
- the company is a member of the Direct Selling Association.

Pensions, insurance and more

Over our working lives, we all seem to amass quite a collection of pensions and insurance policies. By 50 you've probably seen some mature and others you've forgotten about completely. It can be good to take stock from time to time to see exactly what you've got.

Choosing a financial adviser

The best way to review your financial affairs is with an independent financial adviser. You have a choice. There are those who will charge you a fee for their help, and others who earn their living from commission on any financial products you decide to buy from them. There is no right or wrong option; you simply need to be aware that you have a choice.

Other than independent advisers there are tied agents. These are people who only sell one provider's products. Many banks work in this way, relying on the fact that their reputation and credibility will outweigh any disadvantage caused by the narrower product range they offer.

To find an independent financial adviser, ask friends and colleagues who they can recommend. You can look up providers on the internet or in directories, but personal recommendation is often better.

Pensions

It's very rare for an adviser to tell you that your pension fund is too big! Most people recognize though that when they stop work, their income will fall. But then so too might their outgoings. Children are usually financially self-sufficient when you reach retirement age and many people of this age no longer have a mortgage.

Pensions can be very complex and need expert interpretation. However, when looking at your pension and what you hope it will deliver, don't forget also to consider:

- how much it will actually cost you to live in old age
- what other assets/investments you will have that might provide income
- the probability of you inheriting before you retire.

Some people get to 50 and panic about their pension provision. They can see a long, poverty ridden retirement and make all kinds of sacrifices to put money into a pension. Clearly you need to think hard before sacrificing today's comforts for tomorrow's pension. You have to strike a happy balance.

It is also worth remembering that a pension is nothing other than a savings plan. Sure you don't usually pay tax on the money going in, but you might pay tax on the money when it comes out as a pension. Pensions are important, but they are not everything!

Insurance

Nobody wants to think of themselves as being old, sick or dead. Yet these are the pictures painted for you by the insurance industry. They want you to save; they want you to pay insurance premiums so that should you fall desperately ill or die prematurely, you or your dependents will not go without.

The reality is though, that the insurance industry is very profitable. Not least because more people pay their premiums without making a claim, than do. Take the premium income and investment returns of your average insurance company, deduct their operating costs and insurance payouts, and you're usually left with a sizeable profit.

If you took out life insurance some years ago, you might be surprised at how much cheaper you can buy it today, even allowing for your being older. There is much more competition now and people are living longer. Both facts have tended to bring down premium rates.

That's not to say you should take the risk of not being insured; that would be, to put it simply, risky. More to the point is that you need to be realistic. You need to take a pragmatic standpoint when signing up for all those policies that protect your family from what might happen.

To put it more bluntly, if your children have grown up, your partner has a good job, and your home is paid for, life insurance is less important for you than it once was. The image of a grieving young widow with three pre-school children is commonly described by the insurance salesman. It's likely that at 50, this is no longer your situation. Consider downsizing your insurance cover, unless you can spare the cash to pay the premiums and want the comfort of being covered for every eventuality.

Richard

After 30 years working in the public sector, Richard was looking forward to retirement. He'd cut back on some luxuries so that he could put more money into his company pension scheme. With the additional voluntary contributions he calculated that when he retired at 60 he and his partner could take a world cruise, then live a very comfortable retirement.

Three months after his 56th birthday, Richard had a massive heart attack and died. His partner says she would have preferred to take that cruise with Richard and forgone some of the pension. She has a point.

How to make your money go further

Spending money can become a habit and sales people are very persuasive. They know that when we hit 50 we become more cautious and what you might call 'sensible'. This makes us more likely to buy things like insurance and other safety features. You sit on the fence then, perhaps too often, err on the side of caution and go for the more expensive option.

Couple this with our generation's concern that technology is leaving us behind and you can see why salespeople like the over 50s. It's perhaps less of an issue for women because they are often more practical about these things.

Sometimes it's good to stop and take check. Do I really need a phone that also records video? Or a five-year warranty on a kettle?

Things you might not really need

We all buy things we don't need and there's nothing wrong with that. It's called consumer choice. What you need to be certain of is that you have made a conscious choice and not simply fallen victim to the eager young salesperson. Here are some examples:

Things insured twice

It's very easy to be tempted to accept the small insurance premium on your new mobile phone. After all, it means you don't lose out if it gets stolen. However, check first that it's not also covered by your household contents insurance. There's no benefit to insuring things twice.

A new car every three years

If you started driving at 17, you'll remember that new cars then had to be carefully run in. That's because the engines were machined to a lower standard than is possible today. After 70,000 miles (approx. 110,000 km) they were on their last legs and becoming expensive to maintain. Rust was another common sight, with most young drivers of necessity adept at repairing holes with glass-fibre paste and wire mesh. Today's cars will run happily for five times the distance and rarely rust unless damaged. Cars last a lot longer than they used to. Don't change quite so often.

Expensive holidays

Luxury hotels are very nice. They are also very similar. You can wake in the morning on your holiday and forget what country you're in until you leave the hotel. Why not be a little more adventurous and find smaller, family run hotels, or even farmhouse B&Bs? In most countries these offer better value, a fantastic experience and the chance to really get to know the country you're visiting. The internet allows you to find them easily. It also enables you to translate their website into English. These can be really good value when combined with a cheap flight. (Remember too that some overseas-based low-cost airlines offer better fares and different destinations to those based in the UK or Ireland.)

Extras

Whenever you buy any gadget, you have the option of paying more for extras. It has always been the case with cars that the extras are where both manufacturer and dealer make their profit. The same is true of computers, home entertainment systems and almost any consumer electronic device. Once you've agreed to buy the basic model, it's actually quite easy to let yourself be talked into some extras. However, stop and think: will you ever use all of the add-ons you're about to buy? Often it's better to buy a better quality basic model and pass on the extras.

Labels

We all give people credit for noticing far more about us than they do. I once heard a businessman saying that he had to have an expensive suit and luggage because otherwise he'd look foolish in the business class lounge at the airport. Yet by buying all the designer labels, he was actually making himself less visible than if he had developed a tasteful, but cheaper style. At 50 you can carry off being an individual. Why not pass on the overpriced brands? If anybody notices, they'll probably wish they had done the same.

Frank

Frank's work took him all over the world. He met business tycoons and advertising creatives; both groups dressed very differently. He was also saving hard for his retirement and had no desire to play fashion games that would erode his ability to save. Frank decided to only wear black: black trousers, jacket, shirts and socks. He bought good quality garments in a variety of styles. Because his wardrobe was all black, he needed fewer clothes because no colours clashed. Frank became known as the 'man in black' and his reputation grew as quickly as his expenditure on clothes reduced!

Pleasures money cannot buy

Paradoxically, the most important things in life cannot be bought. You acquire them through positive interaction with other people and your environment. Here are some examples:

- **True love.** Those deep, lasting relationships do not need money to create or maintain. Love cannot be bought with expensive gifts. Sex is free too, although of course some do choose to buy it!
- **Good health.** It sounds like a cliché, but people who have little, work hard and stay healthy. People with lots of money are often tempted to over-indulge and damage their health. Money doesn't buy good health.
- **Close friends.** It is shared experience, hope, fear and ambition that bring friends together. The more interests you have in common, the easier it is to become and remain close friends. In fact, by lending and borrowing from friends, you will spend less too!

- **Happiness.** Money cannot buy a state of mind. Both extreme poverty and wealth can undermine happiness. Experiences can make you happy in a way that things never can.
- **The world.** Take the time to be outdoors and watch a sunset. The changing colours can be breathtaking. It costs nothing to view and every sunset is different. Notice nature and you'll be less inclined to spend your money on distractions.
- **A good reputation.** How you behave dictates how people view you, not how you spend. It's a pleasure to have a good reputation, not a cost.
- **Long life.** You might not be looking forward to old age, but the alternative is far less appealing! You cannot buy longevity.

Why some people seem to have more than you

First you have to accept that some people will have more money than you. They may earn more, have inherited more or have very generous benefactors.

Others however simply look as if they have more. There's a wonderful American saying, 'big hat: no cattle' which sums it up perfectly. Here is an example of someone you might meet who falls into that category.

Greg

Greg is the guy next door. He has a house just like yours, a wife and kids just like you and a similar job to you as a middle manager in the public sector. You reckon you probably earn similar amounts and are in fact almost the same age too. You attended his 50th birthday party last year.

What irritates you is that Greg seems to be far better off than you. He drives a new BMW that he changes every year. He has also told you that he has six buy-to-let terraced houses, which you reckon must be worth close to a million.

You on the other hand drive a Ford, have paid off your mortgage and are starting to save a few thousand a year for your old age. You are happy to be debt free, but can't help but think about Greg's wealth and, all those rents he must pocket every month.

Greg is a classic 'big hat: no cattle' man. What you don't know is that he doubled the mortgage on his home to raise the deposit for his first two buy-to-let houses. All three have 90 per cent mortgages and as they've increased in value, Greg has increased the borrowing to release the deposits for the additional four houses.

He has set this up as a company, because he reckons it will help protect him should his 'house of cards' collapse. Through the company he leases the BMW. The rents just about cover the borrowing and the BMW.

His wife is anxious about the debt secured against their home and has worked out that if interest rates rise by 2 per cent they'll end up on the street. She is considering divorcing Greg because she thinks he's taking too big a risk with her future.

Ask yourself: how many Gregs do you know? You can never, ever guess at the reality behind someone else's apparent financial success. It's largely to do with our attitudes to risk. Some like to have little debt and a cash cushion in the bank. Others will risk everything and feel quite comfortable about it. There is no right answer; you have to do what feels right for you.

Action plan: sorting out your finances for your 50s

At 50 you are already experienced at handling money. What's more the inflation you've seen over your lifetime means you are now handling much bigger sums than you once did. It's quite likely that it costs you more today to post a letter than you received as weekly pocket money 40 years ago.

However, 50 is a turning point in your life and you want to make the most of this decade. Here is a checklist to help you make your money go further.

- **Cost goals.** Goal-setting was covered in Chapter 02 so if you made notes then, you might want to turn back to them. What will it cost you to make those dreams come true? Find out exactly how much you'll need and write it down.
- **Check your expenditure.** Look at all the outgoings you currently have. Are there things you could cut out? Have you got the best possible mortgage deal? Are you paying too much for insurances? Check everything.

- **Look ahead.** It may seem heartless to do this, but if you expect to inherit one day, this has to be factored in. There's less need to save for a round the world trip if your 90-year-old favourite aunt has promised to leave you everything. In fact, discussing your planned trip with her will make you feel much better about it when the time comes!

- **Consolidate debts.** Repayment of debts is a potential financial minefield. Take a look at all the small print and interest rates. Consider rolling all your debts, including credit cards, into one loan. The cheapest way to achieve this is to increase your mortgage, but you should take professional advice before doing so.

- **Set a household budget.** Look at what you're spending and where the money goes. If the discovery that you're going through £50 a month on take-out lattes surprises you, decide if it's what you want. Remember that we all have different perceptions of value and need. Don't let others impose their value judgements on you. Decide for yourself what is realistic.

- **Have a savings plan.** Try to get into the habit of regular saving. Even if it's as simple as moving money each month from current to savings account at your bank. Save for a purpose, not just a 'rainy day'.

- **Review regularly.** Make a point of regularly checking your finances. It's not the most exciting way to spend a Sunday afternoon, but it will make sure you stay on track.

- **Remember to consider the risks.** What would you do if long-term sickness or redundancy changed your financial situation?

Finally, remember that money itself has no value. It's what you buy with it that delivers the value. That's why it's important to manage your money well. Quite simply, it allows you to do more of the things you want.

09

managing at work

In this chapter you will learn:
- how to counter ageism
- ways to manage your boss
- how to enjoy work more as you get older.

One way or another you've probably been working for around 30 years. Over those three decades you'll have witnessed countless changes. Technology is perhaps the most obvious thing that has changed. From computers in the office to satellite navigation in the lorry cab, the modern workplace is bristling with equipment we could barely have imagined possible when we were boys.

There have been other, more subtle changes in the workplace over the years. Equality, diversity, work–life balance, health and safety are all topics where you will have witnessed significant shifts in attitude over the years.

If you have kept up with the changes and cheerfully developed the skills you need to keep up, then you're on top of the game. If, however, you have tended to cling to the past, to shun the new and to cynically dismiss political correctness as a passing phase, you may find yourself viewed as a workplace dinosaur.

In other words, as you plan to make life better at work, you need to start with yourself. Have you become stale and somewhat jaded? Or are you the first to try something new? For most of us, work will remain a fact of life for at least another ten years and probably longer. The boundaries between work and retirement are likely to blur even further over the coming years. Work is likely to remain important to you for a while yet.

Ageism and how to avoid it

Increasingly, legislation is driving a change in employer attitudes to older people. It's not uncommon these days to see supermarket checkout operators in their 60s and maybe even older. It is widely recognized that many customer-facing jobs are in fact better done by older people; they have more life experience and that helps.

As you move through your 50s, particularly if you haven't reached a senior position in your organization, you may begin to feel increasingly vulnerable and isolated. Here are some tips to help you combat ageism in your place of work.

- **Don't blame your age.** It's too easy to blame any shortcomings, for example forgetfulness, on your age. If you do, you are simply reinforcing ageist beliefs in the minds of those around you. The truth is that everyone forgets things, not just people aged over 50!

- **Open your mind.** The world is changing and nothing you do or say will take us back to where we were. You need to be open-minded about new developments at work. Greet them with enthusiasm, not the statement that, 'we tried that before and it didn't work then'. The truth is that times change and yesterday's failure can often be repeated as today's success.

- **Look after yourself.** If you've worn the same, favourite tie to work for the past ten years, if your belt is struggling to keep your tummy in its place, if you persist in combing your few remaining strands over the bald patch, then you're going to look old and run down. That's not to say you need to become a fitness freak and wear the latest fashions. It's more that you need to make more effort to look good as you grow older.

- **Keep learning.** Don't let new technology or practices leave you behind. Learning these days is flexible and fun. People in their 80s buy a PC and become skilled in their use. If school for you was an unhappy experience, put things right now with some part-time study. Read the manual for the new photocopier over lunch one day and become the office expert. It won't be that difficult and will earn you respect from your younger peers.

- **Experiment.** Any task quickly becomes a routine. Explore alternatives all the time. Be inquisitive and question the status quo. You'll find that your age gives you the confidence to take the lead and be first to experiment. Gain a reputation as a pioneer and you'll find yourself invited to pilot new things at work.

- **Accept progress.** Most new things in the workplace, be they processes or policies, are usually designed to make life easier. Don't knock them for that; accept that progress means change and go with the flow. If you're the boss, make sure you're not unwittingly holding your organization back by rejecting the new to hang on to the familiar.

Albert

Now in his 70s, Albert runs his own business making signs. His products are used by hospitals and universities to help people navigate large campuses. He employs 20 people but is reluctant to let go of control.

He runs his business from a first floor office which has a window overlooking the workshop. Little escapes his notice. He doesn't know how to use computers, although his admin team use them for typing letters and doing the books. His office is wood panelled, has a large desk with phone and blotter and more often than not smells of cigar smoke.

As Albert's customers retire (and most of them are getting to that age), their replacements find Albert difficult to relate to. They invariably take a look around and find a supplier that seems more up-to-date.

What Albert has not realized, is that if he'd kept up with the times, his new young customers would have grown to respect his vast experience and marvel at his anecdotes from the past. Instead, his family persuaded him to retire and a new MD was hired to take his place.

Out went the wood panelling and heavy desk and in came a meeting table and laptop. The company invested in a website and updated all of its internal systems. Albert benefits financially from the improvement in his firm's fortunes, but still can't quite work out where he went wrong.

Age discrimination

Although legislation exists to prevent discrimination against people because of their age, it still happens. Being overlooked for promotion, forced to retire or switch to part-time work are just two examples of age discrimination you might encounter.

If you think you are being unfairly discriminated against at work, because of your age or for any other reason, you should seek advice. Your employer probably has a defined grievance procedure which is usually a good place to start. If this proves unsatisfactory you might wish to consider taking your case to an employment tribunal. There is no upper age limit for doing this and many solicitors now undertake these cases on a 'no win, no fee' basis. You are probably better to use a local firm of solicitors than respond to one of the national firms that advertise for clients.

How to manage a younger boss

When I was 30 I became a manager for the first time. One of my team, George, was then 55 and somewhat stuck in his ways. I was naïve and he was a seasoned campaigner for his own cause. We battled for a year, with both of us becoming totally miserable as a result. I learned some tough lessons about management and George applied for early retirement. We both lost out. Young bosses don't always know the answers and often need the help of those they manage to succeed.

In theory, this should make the relationship work all the better. In reality, it simply undermines the young manager's confidence. It can also position the older subordinate in the boss's mind as a threat. Being seen as a threat makes it difficult for the relationship to work and so problems arise.

It's also easy for you or me to forget that when we were 20 years younger than we are today, those currently 20 years younger than us were children. In other words if you are 50 and your boss is 30, when you were 30 he or she was only ten years old. That fact is not one your younger boss will thank you for reminding them of. It simply serves to make them feel more vulnerable.

The differences you need to recognize

Your younger boss will be quite different to you, just as you are quite different to them. Here are some of the factors you need to recognize before working on your relationship with them.

- **You've lived longer.** You have seen more, experienced more, and have learned to cope with your world. You probably didn't notice yourself becoming more worldly wise, but it starts when you no longer run for the bus. Put simply, you realize that the next bus will also get you to your destination on time!

- **You have had long-term relationships.** The chances are you've been in some pretty long-term relationships. These help you develop the ability to compromise and adapt to cater for the needs, ideals and sometimes whims of others. Your boss may not be so well established in life!

- **You're probably not as ambitious.** We start our careers with plans to conquer the world. Almost anything seems possible and we throw ourselves at every opportunity that catches our eye. In our 50s, we're more pragmatic about our potential to achieve. By no means over the hill or past ambition, at 50 you're just more realistic about what you want to achieve.

- **You might be resentful.** Like it or not, we tend to get jealous when people younger than ourselves do better than us. It makes us feel somehow as if we've failed, or are inferior. Feelings of resentment, however small, can undermine your relationship with the boss.

How to make the relationship work

When you find yourself working for a young boss, you need to take the initiative if the relationship is to work. That's not to say you should undermine their authority, more that you'll be more aware of how both you and they are feeling. A young boss has not been your age so can't possibly know what it feels like!

Here's a checklist to help you make the relationship work:

- **Show respect.** If you're in a mixed-age team, the younger members will naturally show less respect than you do. That's a feature of your relative maturity. However, if you fail to show enough respect, this will be seen as disrespect, particularly by your peers. Without deferring to the boss unreasonably, make a point of showing respect and being supportive.

- **Deliver the goods.** Young people throw themselves at work challenges with frantic vigour. You on the other hand will be more likely to pace yourself, avoid some of the blind alleys and steadily work things through. Your more deliberate approach to problem solving might be interpreted as a lack of enthusiasm. Make a point of explaining why you choose to work as you do. Illustrate your account with examples of past successes.

- **Work smart.** There is no doubt that at 50 you are less physically resilient than you were two decades before. You may be fitter, but you won't have the same potential for repetitive physical exertion. Make sure, if your job puts physical demands on you, that your boss understands that you might not have the strength or stamina of a younger man.

- **Describe what you feel.** Your boss can only guess at what it feels like to be your age. They may even have had negative experiences of working with people in their 50s. It's up to you to invest time and effort in describing what the world of work looks like to you.

- **Be a team player.** If everyone in the team is younger than you, you might find it difficult to fit in. The important thing for you to recognize is that you don't have to do the things they do, particularly after work. However, you do need to contribute to the team spirit in ways that are comfortable for you, and recognized by them. For example, if the boss takes the team for drinks after work on Friday and you don't drink, volunteer to be the one who drives back afterwards.

Jack and Samantha

Jack is 57 and works for Samantha who is 32. Both work for a car hire firm, with Samantha being manager of the branch where they both work. When Samantha arrived, Jack had worked there for five years. He dealt with the larger customers, making sure they kept their business with the firm.

Once Samantha had settled in, Jack suggested they go out for lunch to talk. He explained that he hoped to retire in two years' time and wanted to make sure that Samantha had all the help from him she needed to make that possible. Jack started introducing Samantha to their larger customers and made sure she came to understand what made them tick.

After a year, Samantha asked Jack if he'd like to stay on part-time after he retired. She would, she told him, welcome his help in keeping the business growing. This gave Jack more choices about retirement than he would otherwise have had.

How you can add more value at work in your 50s

It's reassuring to know that researchers have found that older employees offer distinct advantages over younger workers. Of course such surveys are quite general and for every advantage attributed to the older worker, you may know someone who doesn't fit the description.

However, it is worth ending this chapter with a look at the benefits your employer might gain from keeping you for as long as possible. Older employees, in general:

- **Go absent less often.** Major sporting events, recovering from heavy nights out, problems with children, all can prompt the younger worker to take time off work when really they shouldn't. Absenteeism is a real problem in some industry sectors. Older people are less likely not to turn up in the morning.
- **Stay with the firm for longer.** Young people are rarely well advised to wait around for promotion opportunities to arise where they are. More they start looking for the next job as soon as they feel able to handle it. Older employees are less likely to be chasing a career and therefore more likely to stay for longer.

- **Show more loyalty.** Young people can be passionate about their job, but only in so far as what it does for them. Older people retain that traditional loyalty to the firm that their parents might have shown.
- **Are more honest.** It's not a pleasant statistic, but in business areas such as retail, where staff dishonesty can be a problem, there is evidence to suggest that older people are less likely to steal from their employer than younger staff.
- **Are more flexible.** Older people are willing to work longer or shorter hours to meet operational needs. Younger workers tend to have more other demands on their time. It is also true to say that many young people today put their personal goals ahead of their work commitments. That's not to say it's wrong, just that younger, particularly single people, will often refuse overtime if it clashes with an important social engagement.

How to decide where the grass is greenest

When relationships at work get a little fraught it's easy to imagine that self-employment might suit you better. The next chapter deals with this and how to do it, but for now, here are some good reasons why you might be better off working for someone else:

Freedom

You might want it to be bigger, but at least as an employee your pay-check arrives on time every month. If you worked for yourself, your income might be higher, but it would also arrive more erratically. Don't underestimate the comfort a regular monthly salary can bring.

Control

If you've built yourself a position of respect within your firm, it can be very nice. People further down the organization carry out the boring tasks that you know you wouldn't enjoy. If you started on your own, you would have to do everything.

Ambition

It's wrong to assume you won't be ambitious at 50; many remain keen to build their career until they are quite old. In the corporate world, there's usually a ladder of sorts to climb.

Pension

However inadequate you think it will be when the time comes, don't sacrifice the company pension scheme without a lot of careful research. If you are lucky enough to have a works pension that will be linked to your final pay, do all you can to keep it. In 30 years' time you'll be glad you did!

Holidays

As an employee you might take work worries with you on holiday, but would you even dare take holidays if you worked for yourself? Many self-employed people don't take holidays, or if they do they tend to be short. Working for someone else you're more likely to have long relaxing holidays.

Action plan: how to enjoy work more in your 50s

You can see from this chapter that at or around 50 you have much to offer your employer. You are more predictable and probably more compliant than your younger colleagues. That's not to say you allow yourself to be exploited, more that you are more mature and understand the quid pro quo.

Here's an action plan to help you enjoy work more:

- **Check your financial goals.** How much do you need or want to earn to do the things you want to do? How long do you want to maintain that level of income?
- **Create a career plan.** This is simply a list of the things you want from work over the remainder of your career. For example, you might want your job to give you:
  - a secure source of income for the next ten years
  - the flexibility to take more time off as you get older
  - one more opportunity to try to reach the top
  - the chance to help develop younger people and pass on your skills and experience.
- **Involve your boss.** However tempting to keep your plans to yourself, sharing with your boss usually makes sense. For one thing, he or she will then understand what you're hoping to do. If your plans for the future conflict, it's probably better to deal with it sooner rather than later.
- **Play your part.** It's easy to simply become the grumpy old man of the office. A more positive role to play is that of

mentor and supporter to those younger than you. If you have children, you can use your parenting skills in the workplace quite effectively. Just make sure it's not too obvious!

Work is viewed by too many of our generation as a necessary evil. This is perhaps a hangover from the attitudes of our fathers' generation. They worked because they felt they had to. They also believed themselves to be somehow tied to their employers and were themselves taught to be grateful for a job. Luckily for us all, life's just not like that any more.

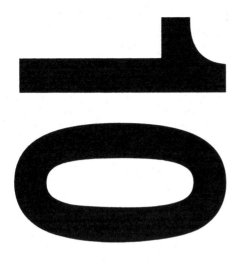

self-employment

In this chapter you will learn:
- the pros and cons of self-employment
- how to plan and start your own business
- where to go for further help and advice.

If you have the urge, the courage and the cash, starting your own business in mid-life can be a great experience. You can leave behind much of what you dislike about work and enjoy a level of autonomy you might currently only dream of.

Each year in the UK some 300,000 people start a business. Many only last a year or two, so you will also see statistics that claim a similar number of business closures each year. Do not confuse these with bankruptcies. More often they are the result of businesses merging together, people retiring or young people simply choosing to get a job after a period of self-employment.

The prospect of self-employment might seem like a distant dream if you've always been employed. This chapter will help you decide if it's for you.

Why more people are starting a business in their 50s

There are many reasons why more new businesses today are being established by people aged over 50. For one thing, there are more of us. (There are significantly more men in the Western world aged 50 to 60 than there are aged 40 to 50.) Another reason is that there has never been more opportunity for the self-employed.

The very reasons that prompt the large corporations to reduce their headcount are also the reasons why there's more work out there for the freelancer. Corporate organizations are increasingly being encouraged to focus on their core activities. Rather than diversifying they are divesting themselves of non-core activities, reducing overhead costs and outsourcing all that they can.

Businesses are started by people of all ages and bookstores are full of useful guides to help them. You though are in your 50s and so will have a slightly different agenda to someone half your age.

Here are some factors that will count in your favour if you decide to go it alone:

Wisdom

Most of us grow wiser as we grow older. Wisdom, grounded in a lifetime's experience, will help you ride out the storms and overcome the obstacles. It is also fair to say that when you run your own business; your customers will think you a safer option than someone younger offering the same product or service. Whereas employers may not always seem to value wisdom and maturity, customers of small firms usually do. To them, maturity equals wisdom, unless you encourage them to think otherwise.

Experience

All experience is useful when you work for yourself. It doesn't matter if you are an experienced engineer running a bookstore, you'll find aspects of your experience invaluable in your new role. In a small business, experience is as much about coping with the unexpected as exploiting time-honed skills.

Tenacity

By the age of 50 you've picked up a few of life's bruises. You'll have made some painful mistakes, suffered loss as well as ecstasy, and developed the resilience to manage. With any small business you encounter more rejections than invitations. The tenacity, or inner strength, you've gained over the years will stop you giving up too easily.

Cash cushion

Many people negotiate their way out of full time employment to start a business. They agree to leave in exchange for an enhanced pension deal. Some jobs, most notably perhaps the police, allow you to retire after 30 years of service, by which time you might not even have reached 50. Having a pension of sorts, together with a comparative freedom from major debt, makes it easier for the over 50s to survive on a lower income whilst they build their new enterprise.

A strong network

The old adage, 'it's not what you know but who', is at its most true when you talk about small businesses. If you start a business you will inevitably find your first customers from within your personal network. (For a surprising number, that first customer is their recent employer!) By the age of 50 you have probably built a good network of contacts, even though you might not realize it.

Keith

After more than 25 years as a health and safety manager in industry, Keith decided that at 52 he needed a change. He'd spent the last ten years cooped up in a cardboard box factory and the annual cycle of audit, advice and staff training was beginning to wear him down.

He considered changing jobs, but realized this would only see him doing the same job in a different factory. His firm was also cutting back on managers as it coped with an industry-wide downturn. He checked out the offer and found he could leave with a respectable lump sum and a modest pension.

He took the money and with help from a government-funded business start-up agency, put together his business plan. He had seen that smaller firms that couldn't afford a health and safety manager were at risk. The law was becoming very strict and he thought he could provide them with the support they needed at a price they could afford.

Keith's first customer was his old firm. They needed him for three days a week for a month. He spent the other days networking and looking for new customers. At first it was slow, but now two years later he is very busy. He now has control of his life, plenty of variety and no boss!

How to go self-employed

As with everything you choose to change about life in your 50s, you have to start by setting some goals. What do you want your business to do? Is it simply going to be a way of making a living from something you love? Or do you have visions of becoming the next Richard Branson? At 50, both are possible, but you have to aim for one, the other, or somewhere you've defined in between. Here are five steps to get you from employed to self-employed:

Step 1 – ask yourself why?

You need to be honest with yourself and work out what's driving this ambition. Are you running towards a goal or away from a nightmare? In times of recession, many people start a business because they can't find a job. As you might imagine, they often come unstuck for one simple reason: they're doing it for the *wrong* reason. Good reasons to start your own enterprise might include:

- **Your employer's handing it to you on a plate.** Perhaps the activity you head up no longer fits, but still has potential. You've been offered the opportunity to buy it out and build it up.
- **You have a skill people want.** You might be a taxidermist or a t'ai chi trainer, it doesn't matter what, but you know people want what you do and are prepared to pay for it.
- **You can see how others are missing the real opportunity.** Your plan is to take something others already do and do it differently. This is arguably the best and most common motivation for starting a business. Few who want to start something that's never been done before actually succeed. In reality, there is little that's new.
- **You can afford to work fewer hours.** In a situation where your employer won't allow you to reduce your hours, you're talking about 'semi-retirement', and therefore your enterprise is going to be relatively low risk. In other words, you want it to make money, but won't be totally reliant on it.

Once you really know why you're doing it, you can then look at how.

Step 2 – ask yourself what?

You next need to work out more precisely what your enterprise will do. Generalities are no good at this stage, you need to be specific. To market your business you will need to be able to sum up what it is you do and why you're different in less than one minute. Few can do this, but you should aim to know exactly what your new business will do. Here are some examples to illustrate the point:

- 'I'm going to specialize in cleaning stair carpets because most contractors won't take them on.'
- 'We will make cheesecakes to order and sell them via the internet. We will be special because we will offer 400 different cheesecakes and will only use organic produce.'
- 'I've spent 25 years checking pressure vessels for invisible cracks. I'll be the only independent contractor doing this with the right certification to work offshore.'

Step 3 – ask yourself where?

Good market research is the secret of success. If you kid yourself, or even your bank manager, that the market's bigger than it is, you will inevitably fall short of your target sales.

You need to be honest with yourself and work out as accurately as you can how big the potential market is for your product or service. It needs to be large enough to meet your needs, which if you are planning a one-man firm is not very large! Many succeed by working in a very specific niche market.

Market research is something of a science and whilst major brand owners carry out very sophisticated market surveys, your research can be a little more down to earth. Here are some research tips to help you define your market.

Where will you trade?
Will you travel the world like Red Adair, or is your marketplace the neighbourhood where you live? Work out your territory and remember that customers probably won't travel too far to find you. Furthermore, travel takes time and costs money; you won't want to travel too far either. Put some figures to your marketplace using:

- population statistics from local government websites
- trade association reports/data
- newspaper and journal advertising rate cards (these define the markets they reach)
- statistics gleaned from academic research papers and libraries.

Who will you trade with?
Define the people who will become your customers. Understand what it is about them that will make them your customers. Knowing what they have in common will help you later when you need to promote yourself to them. Even if your product or service has universal appeal (say you're opening a bakery), understand the demographics of your marketplace by:

- walking the streets and talking to people (if you're going to trade locally)
- attending trade fairs and conventions
- library and internet research.

Why will they buy?
You need to really know why they will buy from you. You do this by defining the gap in the market you hope to fill. Ideally, there are already suppliers of the product or service you will provide. You need to work out how you're going to be different and what this means in terms of benefits to your customer. This is arguably the most important part of your research, for

without a reason to buy from you, people won't. Here are some things you can do to define your market position:

- 'mystery shop' those you plan to compete with
- read research and survey documents that describe market trends in your chosen sector
- talk to people about their experiences and frustrations.

Step 4 – ask yourself how?

Having worked out your motivation, ambition and the size of opportunity, you now need to pull it all together in a business plan. This is the document that will chart your journey through the first year or so of your new enterprise.

There are plenty of business plan templates to choose from. Most banks will give you a guide to writing your business plan. You can also download templates from their websites. The spreadsheets are particularly useful, if only because you don't have to create all the complicated formulae yourself!

Perhaps the most important thing to remember about your business plan is that you are writing it for you. It is your plan, for your enterprise and your future. Too often, business plans are written to impress a bank manager. That is actually a different challenge that might require a different version of your own plan.

Your business plan needs to:

- be concise and focused, ideally no more than four sides of A4 paper
- define the opportunity you plan to exploit
- set both short- and long-term objectives
- detail the skills, experience and resources you have
- predict cash flow and profitability for the first year at least
- set out how you will attract and retain customers
- show how you will monitor progress
- define your exit strategy – who will buy your business and why when you want to stop.

Step 5 – ask yourself when?

Actually, there is no ideal time to start a business. If it's in you to do it, then you need to do it sooner rather than later. Too much time planning and you'll talk yourself out of making a move. Delay can also increase your sense of frustration with work and that can lead to problems. You need to start your business with the right attitude: positive, assertive and enthusiastic. Here are some factors to consider when deciding when:

- **What's just around the corner?** Is there new legislation looming that will fuel demand for your new business? Is one of the current suppliers about to go bust or sell out? Dig out that market intelligence and use it to decide when.

- **What about your job?** There's no point in leaving your employer in the lurch. After all, many people find that their first big customer is their former employer. However much you hate work, you need to make sure you leave on good terms.

- **What about money?** You need money to start a business, if only to cover your living expenses whilst you get established. Have you got an insurance policy maturing soon? Is it worth waiting a while for your pension to reach a critical point? Does your age make a difference? Are you likely to be made redundant soon, in which case why not wait for the offer?

- **How does it fit with your family's plans?** Are your children about to go to university? Have you other expenses on the horizon? Your new enterprise needs to dovetail into your life, not be an extra challenge at an already challenging time.

Common mistakes and how to avoid them

Because so many people start a business every year, almost every mistake you can make has already been made by someone else. You can benefit from this and avoid perhaps some of the pitfalls that await the unwary.

Don't kid yourself that you or your new enterprise are any different. Everyone makes mistakes and no business is unique. Here are some common mistakes and how to avoid them:

Over-preparing
You keep putting off the search for customers as you seek to prepare every aspect of your business first. It is important to be prepared, but actually you need customers to help you do that. Your initial customers will tell you what they expect and will also point out the flaws in your systems. It's always better to start with a demanding customer who helps you shape your business, than spend months preparing before letting a customer near!

Under-funding

Your business plan shows some bold projections and your cash flow will, you anticipate, be healthy. Reality, however, often differs from expectation. If you don't have enough cash or access to debt and the business takes off more slowly than you thought, you've got problems. Better to have too much funding than not enough. Ways to plan funding better include:

- prepare several cash flow forecasts; look at the impact of customers paying you late (they will) and sales coming in slowly (they might)
- consider offering a discount for cash with order
- negotiate late payment with your suppliers
- don't forget VAT and other taxes you have to collect/pay.

The wrong people

It's easy to go into business with the wrong people. Family and friends might not be the most objective. Choose your business partners carefully and have a written agreement. If you hit a rough patch, falling out will be easy. Pre-empt disagreement by having the relationship defined and recorded.

Over-spending

Can you remember when you first set up home? You probably borrowed stuff, bought second-hand, improvised and went without. It's the same with your business. Don't be tempted to spend money you can't really spare on things you don't really need.

Sell, sell sell

You'll find plenty of distracting forms to fill in and tasks to do if you look for them. The truth is you need to spend your time selling and everything else should come second. Always put customers first.

Listen

Customers and those who choose not to do business with you provide valuable feedback. If you're selling pink ones and they want green, don't ignore their demands. Adapt to meet your customers' needs.

Don't over-trade

This is a rather technical term to describe growing too fast. Basically what happens is that you are more successful than you anticipated. Orders flood in and you buy lots of stock to meet the surging demand. You reach a point where you suddenly find you have no money in the bank, are owed lots but need it right now. Over-trading is one of the major causes of business failure. You need to learn to say no.

Under-promise and over-deliver

Reputation is the gap between your expectation and that of your customer. Promise too much and they feel let down if you don't then deliver. Promise just enough and you can delight them by providing just a little more.

> **Joshua**
>
> Finding that his race was handicapping his career prospects, Joshua decided to start his own business. He had always been interested in Caribbean food and had many of his grandmother's recipes in an old book she had given him as a child. He decided to start a restaurant to give people in the city he lived in a chance to taste the dishes he so fondly remembered from his youth.
>
> There was one street that had a range of ethnic restaurants and most seemed to do well. One had become vacant and seemed to be in a good location. His research also revealed that in six months' time, there was going to be a major arts festival in the city, focusing on Afro-Caribbean culture. He thought he could link the opening of his restaurant to that festival and made contact with the organizers.
>
> They asked him to join an organizing committee and this gave him the chance to raise his profile. He wrote his business plan, got the support of his bank and opened for business on the first day of the arts festival. He hosted a party for the festival organizers and the press. This gave him lots of good reviews and the phone started to ring. He is now full every night and making good money.

People who can help you become an entrepreneur

Starting a business is a lonely affair and the more people you have supporting you, the better your chances of success. Some, such as customers are obvious, but others are less so. Here is a selection:

- **Your partner.** The person you share your life with has a huge role to play. If you have children still at home, so do they. You need their love and support more than ever if you're going to start a business.

- **The bank.** Your bank manager, or the bank manager who finally says yes to your plan, is important to your success. Keep them involved and up-to-date with how things are going. Never keep your bank manager in the dark.
- **Your boss.** Never, ever underestimate the extent to which your boss can help you. If they understand why you're doing it, and you've worked together to minimize the impact of your departure, they can often introduce you to business.
- **Your network.** The people you know may not be in a position to become your customers. They may know people who can though. Actively seek introductions through your social and business networks.
- **Heroes.** We all have heroes. Who has succeeded that you really admire? Are they well known names, in which case you can read their story in books? Perhaps they are simply local business people you admire, in which case you can flatter them into becoming your mentor.
- **Your competitors.** As a business grows, it usually finds that its customers change too. Whereas in the early years you have time for the small, demanding customer, as you grow they become harder to service. Sometimes, competitors will happily pass you the smaller business that you can profit from, but they cannot.

Alf

Alf spent the first 30 years of his career working for a company that installed animal feed mills. When he was 51, his employer sold out to a larger rival and the company culture changed. Alf did not like this so decided to start his own business, focusing on the smaller feed mills his new employer was less interested in servicing.

Alf started his business 30 years ago. He is now 81 and still works four days a week, because he says he loves it. The company diversified over the years, but still designs, installs and commissions materials handling equipment in feed mills, bakeries and large steel-making plants.

Having started his business at an age when many are thinking of slowing down, he has enjoyed a long and successful second career.

Action plan: taking the plunge

Inertia and fear are probably the two things holding you back. Both need to be overcome if you are to successfully start your own business. Both however are also useful, encouraging you to be cautious and not take silly risks. In your 50s, you should be more risk averse as you probably have more to lose. It's also harder in mid-life to pick yourself up after a fall and start the game again. Here's one final list on self-employment to help you if you're stuck on the fence and cannot decide what to do.

- **Map two routes.** Write a business plan and also a 'staying in your job' plan. Imagine the journey both routes could give you. Literally map these out on the same large piece of paper so that you can easily refer across. Which looks best in two and five years' time? Are the risks greater if you stay working, or if you go it alone?

- **Argue against your plan.** Have your partner or a friend present your plan to you. Your role is to pick holes in it and be as negative as you can. Get out all of your concerns and see how the other person overcomes the objections. Then remember that it's your plan. If someone else can robustly defend it, think how much better you will be able to do this.

- **Don't stay on the fence too long.** Set yourself a time limit by when you will have made up your mind. Once you've decided, don't re-visit the debate. No one makes major life decisions with the benefit of hindsight. Don't beat yourself up if subsequent events suggest you should have acted differently. That's life!

redundancy

In this chapter you will learn:
- why redundancy isn't always bad
- what to do if it happens to you
- how to find another job.

For many of us, redundancy in our 50s is a major fear. Having got over the fear of being considered too old at 40, reaching 50 brings it all back again. What makes it worse is that pension legislation means you can actually retire at 50. That is if you have enough cash in the fund to do this.

As many large organizations downsized in the 1990s, people aged 50 or over found themselves being offered a deal to take early retirement. Some who took this option did actually retire, potentially facing 40 years of doing nothing. More decided to make the most of the situation and start a new career.

Why redundancy can be an opportunity

The longer you work for an organization the more it will cost them to make you redundant. However, that cost is offset by the fact that younger people are often paid less. There are countless laws designed to protect the rights of the employee when he or she finds themselves in a job that is to become redundant (technically it's the post not the person that goes). In reality though, whilst an employer will make sure they comply with all the relevant legislation, the decision to move you on may seem quite arbitrary.

Redundancy though can give you that little push you need to change your life. We all become settled into the routine of life and work and whilst redundancy disrupts that, it also brings with it opportunities. Here are a few to illustrate the point:

Downsize

If you're in a high pressure, high salary job you might actually welcome the opportunity to downsize. Many men find they need less income in their 50s. This coupled with a growing concern that old age is getting just a little closer, prompts many of us to re-examine how we spend our time.

Redundancy gives you a complete break with the old and the chance of a fresh start. There's no reason why you should not take two part-time jobs and only work four days a week.

Re-train

If you've always wanted to be a truck driver, why not take it up now? If you've worked indoors for the last 30 years, perhaps an outdoor job would make a pleasant change. As governments become more conscious of the growing need to keep the over 50s economically active, many re-training schemes are free to attend. There are also jobs that really lend themselves to our age group. Counsellors and the like tend to be easier to talk to if they are mature rather than young.

Re-locate

If you've stayed in the city for your job, but hanker after life in the country, redundancy can give you the break you need. You might also find that you can move house and have cash left over. This also gives you greater freedom as you plan your future.

For many men, particularly those that have been with the same employer a long time, redundancy can be a real shock. In fact you may also experience the physical and psychological symptoms of shock. Depression in particular can strike at a time when you need your wits about you to find new employment. If you think you have become depressed, consult your doctor.

Oscar

Since his sons were young, Oscar had helped with the local scout group. He had led many expeditions and had qualified as a canoeing instructor.

When his employer, a large double-glazing manufacturer lost a major contract they cut out a layer of management. Oscar's job was one of those that disappeared. The thought of finding another management job in manufacturing didn't exactly enthral Oscar and he knew that at 53 this would not be easy anyway.

Then he noticed an advertisement in his local paper for youth workers. The money was less than he had been earning, but then so were the hours. He applied and found his interviewer shared his interest in scouting. He was offered the job and finds he is enjoying work now more than he has for years. Oscar's pleased his job disappeared!

Why redundancy can also be a threat

Despite all the opportunities, of course there are also threats posed by redundancy. It would be misleading to ignore them. Redundancy can be a real blow. Here are some of the negative results that redundancy can prompt.

Depression

However positively you might be encouraged to view redundancy, it is always to some extent taken as rejection. If you've been working long and hard, making sacrifices for your job and then it's taken away, it hurts. It's quite natural to feel depressed when made redundant. However, you also need to be aware there's a fine line between that and clinical depression. Depression is an illness and if it grabs you, needs treating. Don't be afraid to consult your doctor if you get depressed.

Money problems

Although many 50-year-olds are comfortably off, many too are not. Children, divorce and simply the cost of living can mean that you more or less live from one pay day to the next. If you've not worked for your current employer very long, your redundancy pay can be modest. This can induce panic as you wonder how you'll manage all the bills.

Relationship problems

It could be that things have not been right between you and your partner. Perhaps you're working through a tough patch. Redundancy then forces you to spend more time at home together. It is also an emotional experience for any partner to see his or her loved one out of work. This can put an additional strain on your relationship, paradoxically at a time when you need a partner's support more than ever before.

However you think you will react to redundancy, when it happens, it's not quite as you expected. Your quite understandable emotional response pushes logic to one side and sets you off on a roller-coaster ride. You veer between the peaks of opportunity and troughs filled with fear.

You can also feel quite alone. It's usual for people to be told and then leave their workplace immediately. You have little opportunity to tidy up loose ends, or to say goodbye to colleagues. Understandably, the people you worked with may also find it difficult to cope with your sudden departure. On the one hand they feel for you and want to offer support. On the other there is relief that it's not them facing redundancy. Loyalties become divided and conversations can be embarrassing. You are very much on your own.

Things you need to know and do

As with any traumatic experience, your first feeling after being told you are being made redundant is one of shock. It's that same shock you might experience if you witness an accident, or hurt yourself. It's your body's way of protecting itself from further pain and distress.

However sensitively you are given the news, or however much you saw it coming, you will be shocked. In fact that shock might be shared by the person tasked with telling you. Unless you've made somebody redundant you won't realize, but doing the deed is far from pleasant and can take a while to get over.

Here then are some things you need to do if you find yourself made redundant:

Avoid anger
It's rarely the fault of the person delivering the message that you're losing your job. There's little to be gained by getting angry with them. In fact there's no point in getting angry at all. It simply upsets you and everyone around you. Try to avoid anger.

Don't take it personally
All the rule books say it's the job and not the person that's no longer required. Even if you are convinced you've been chosen for redundancy for all the wrong reasons, try not to take it personally. Even if it is personal, it's not a criticism of your very being, more that for whatever reason you no longer fitted.

Take time out
However much you think you're being rational about it, emotion will be clouding your judgement. It's really important during the first week or so to take time out to reflect, think, plan and discuss. Hasty decisions may not always be the best ones.

Tie up loose ends
Even though the chance seems remote at the time, it's surprisingly common for people to find their new role through their old employer. If you're asked to stay a while and tidy loose ends, do it. If nothing else you want a good reference, don't you?

Check the figures
Go through the offer you've been made and make sure all you're entitled to has been included. It is unlikely that your employer would try to short-change you. There is a chance that someone

has miscalculated the figures. There are plenty of useful reference websites that can help you understand what you are entitled to. Don't forget holiday pay!

Think before you complain

You don't want to be a pushover, but equally engaging a 'no win no fee' lawyer to hound your former employer in an industrial tribunal might not help you in the long term. Tribunals are time consuming, emotionally draining and scrupulously fair. Unless you have clearly been abused in some way, a tribunal might not be the best route to go. Often it's better to accept what has happened and move on.

Manage your debts

We all owe money. The people we owe are called creditors. Yours might include a mortgage lender and some credit card companies. If you think you're going to find money tight for a few months, talk to the lenders straight away. Never put off telling people you're in trouble.

You will be far from the first person to face these same problems. Most banks, building societies and even utilities companies have teams who advise people who find themselves unable to pay. They can usually work out a way for you to avoid defaulting and getting a bad credit record.

Claim benefits

If you've never been made redundant before, you won't know what you might be entitled to in terms of government benefit. Remember that you've been paying tax so really, all you're doing is asking for some of it back. There is no stigma attached to redundancy and unemployment. Find out what you are entitled to and ask for it.

Take a holiday

A week on the beach might be farthest from your mind, but it is often the best thing to do. Once you've dealt with the immediate fallout of your redundancy, take your partner and go somewhere nice. Force yourself to take a break and relax. If nothing else, it will make it easier for you to find another job. You've had a tough time, you deserve a holiday.

Deciding what to do with the rest of your life

You may not have chosen the timing, but you can choose what to do next. For most people, finding another job will be their priority, but this is not the only option. Here are some alternatives you might consider, if only in passing, as you plan your next move.

Self-employment

If you work for yourself, you are highly unlikely to face redundancy. However this should not your only motive for working for yourself. Chapter 10 of this book introduces you to the concept of self-employment. It also encourages you to ask yourself the questions that might help you make the best choice. Self-employment is not for everybody, but for some redundancy gives them the gentle nudge they need in that direction.

Volunteering

If you received a generous payoff, you might be able to afford to take time off to travel. Many aid agencies are now recruiting people in their 50s for short assignments in the developing world.

Volunteering can give you a fresh perspective on life and invigorate you after years in the workplace. If you can afford to take the time out, this will also make you more employable when you return home.

Voluntary sector

Many managers working in the charity sector moved there in mid-life. The skills needed are broadly similar to those in the private and public sector. The money is less and, with the exception of the very large charities, organizations are poorly resourced.

However, the voluntary sector exists to meet needs that otherwise would not be met. You can usually find an organization that works in an area you have some feeling for. That makes it easier to accept the lower salary. Working in the voluntary sector also helps you to feel you are contributing something to society. For many, this is important, particularly as we age.

Job hunting in your 50s

If you've decided to get a new job, then you already have one. It's called getting a new job. The more you can treat your job search as a job, the more easily you will find a new post. This is because you will be more disciplined and organized, not to say more businesslike, if you approach the task as you would a project at work.

Your first task then is to set up your home office, unless you already have one. This is where you will spend at least half of every working day looking for work, except of course when you have an interview! Your office needs to have a PC or laptop with internet access and a phone. The chances are you have this already, but note that it also needs to be quiet. Barking dogs or screaming children do not create the best impression when you're talking to a prospective employer.

Here's how to set about finding yourself a new job:

Define what you offer

You need to work out exactly what it is you have to offer a new employer. It's not just the list of achievements you'll write on your CV – it's much more than that.

> **Khalid**
> Khalid has spent all of his life in the motor trade, with some workshop and some sales experience. For the last five years he was a branch manager. What does this really mean? Well it means he can work unsupervised and is comfortable being responsible for budgets, profitability and people. Those skills don't just apply to the motor trade, but to many other businesses.

Scope your opportunity

In the example above, Khalid might be tempted to just look for work in the motor trade. He would probably end up taking a step back and work as a car salesman, on a commission-based deal. In fact, he can do much better than that. He can manage any operation of the size and complexity of the dealership branch he was running when he was made redundant.

You need to do the same. Look at your track record and see where else it might be applied. Be creative when you explore the options and perhaps scan the job ads for ideas. Don't simply think you need to work in the industry you worked in before.

Write a CV

Your CV is your selling document or prospectus. It tells a prospective employer what you can offer and why they should meet you. Because recruiters see lots of CVs, you can make life easier for them, for example:

- keep it short and factual: aim for no more than two pages of A4
- start with a paragraph that sums up what you offer and why you are worth employing – it's often useful to write this in the 'third person', as if the reader is saying the words themselves (for example, 'Khalid is an experienced team leader ... etc.)
- avoid fancy typefaces or coloured paper. Binding your CV into a folder simply means the recruiter has to tear it out to distribute
- when laying out your CV, list your most recent post first and in more detail than you describe earlier roles
- be honest about your age – give both date of birth and age; also comment on your health and fitness (any recruiter will want to know)
- enclose a professionally taken photograph – this will enable the recruiter to see in a flash that you are not a tired, overweight old man in a scruffy suit (and if you're worried that this describes you, wear flattering clothes and have a haircut before the photo is taken!)
- use your list of interests to show as wide a range of activities as possible (if you're 59 and a coach with your local running club, put it down; it shows just how energetic you are!)
- try to embed within your CV facts that illustrate your comfort with modern business practice and technology – a young recruiter may assume you to be a Luddite unless you show that you're not
- be easy to contact – give your home and mobile phone numbers and an email address; if your home email address is humorous, get a new one just for your job seeking (recruiters might be reluctant to email an interview offer to oldfart@hotmail.com!).

Most important of all have a master copy that is your basic CV. From this you can adapt your CV to meet the specific needs of each job you apply for. Keep copies of each version so that you can refer to it at interview.

Finding jobs

Of course you will send your CV to every recruitment agency you can find, as well as reading national and local newspapers. You might also look at relevant trade magazines and there are numerous jobs websites.

These are the obvious places to look. There are also less obvious ways to find jobs to apply for. These include:

Networking

Make sure everyone you know is aware that you are looking for a new job. Don't embarrass your contacts by asking them to hire you. Instead, ask them to make introductions to people they know. It's often the people you know least well who give you the best introductions.

Your old firm

Colleagues, suppliers and customers all have the potential to make valuable introductions. It's tempting to keep a low profile when you're made redundant. This is neither necessary nor is it desirable. Don't be pushy, but do be in touch.

News stories

Behind many news headlines are job opportunities. Firms winning new contracts or organizations taking on new functions often need new people. If you've always worked for large firms, don't overlook the potential to work for a small company. Owner managers can respond very well to an unsolicited letter prompted by a recent good news story.

John

After two years of job searching in the depths of the last recession, John got really fed up. He was now 55 and it seemed as though he would never get a job. He wasn't even fussy what he did. All he wanted was to have a job that gave him a living wage and his self-respect back.

Then one afternoon he had an idea. He had some sandwich boards made that said, 'Can you give me a job?' and phoned the local newspaper to tell them his plan. The reporter and photographer found him the next morning standing at a roundabout in the town centre in the rush-hour traffic. The boards were certainly attracting attention and the newspaper printed his story the next day.

Three employers saw the story, admired John's enterprise and phoned the paper. One of them offered John a job. He is now very happy.

Getting an interview

The key to getting an interview is to make sure your CV lands on the right desk and is noticed. If you're writing on spec to firms you read about in the paper, then you are automatically on a short list of one. They will either contact you and talk, ignore you, or just maybe write to say 'thanks but no thanks'.

When you are applying for an advertised job, your application will need to stand out from the others. Your CV will go some way towards achieving this, as will a photograph. Most important of all is the covering letter. This is what the recruiter will use for their initial selection. A poor letter with errors and you're straight in the 'no' pile. A good letter and you're on the maybe pile for further consideration.

Here are some tips for writing that letter of application:

- **Get names right.** It's easy when you're making lots of applications to get names muddled up. Be sure to also spell names correctly and avoid using archaic titles such as esq.

- **Use their reference number.** If they have a job reference number, put it in the address or on the envelope. It lets whoever is doing the initial sort get you into the right pile.

- **One page only.** No application letter should run to two pages – the recruiter will probably not bother to read beyond the first one.

- **Use their words.** The more of their words you can include in the letter, without going over the top, the more they will relate to it. Those key words in the ad (for example, flexible, energetic, enthusiastic) may well have been derived from the meeting where the person specification was drawn up. Using them means you are saying you fit that profile exactly.

- **Sign in colour.** A very small point, but signing your letter in a colour other than black shows that you've really signed it and not simply mail merged this letter with 100 others.

Having sent the letter (or emailed it) you then need to wait. Sometimes it can be worth a follow-up phone call. At other times this will turn off the recruiter, as you appear too keen. Play each one by ear and make your decision job by job.

The interview

So much about the interview depends on the job you're applying for, your background and your personal style. In your 50s, no one should expect you to be as conformist as you might have been at 30. However, you do need to strike a happy balance between being individualistic and being too grey.

It also might be the case that you've not attended a job interview for decades. This can make you overly nervous as you will almost inevitably feel uncomfortable and vulnerable. Here are some top interview tips to help you succeed:

- **Don't act old.** Recognize that there is less formality in business these days and be relaxed. If you act formally in an interview it can become increasingly uncomfortable. The interviewer will feel this more than you do. It won't help you get the job.

- **Look the part.** Make an effort with your appearance but don't try too hard. Remember that short hair is always better than long. Dyed hair is going to look obvious and, for most people, beards don't make them appear youthful. Wear a bright tie.

- **Be gentle.** It's possible you'll know more about the subjects discussed than the interviewers. You need to make sure they feel comfortable with you and not undermined by your superior experience! If they dry up (and interviewers sometimes do) ask them a question or two about the job to give them a chance to recover.

- **Watch the clock.** It's obvious that you need to make sure you arrive on time, have time to visit the toilet and generally calm down before the interview. It is equally important to be businesslike and find out how long the interview is expected to last. Play your part in making it keep to time. Remember that receptionists and secretaries are often asked for their opinions on the candidates they've greeted.

- **Summarize.** At the end, it can be helpful to summarize the key points you've covered together. It's also good to ask if they have any nagging doubts that need clearing up. Ask this in a light-hearted way as it could be that things like your state of health or retirement plans are on their mind, but they're too polite to ask outright.

- **Smile as you leave.** The ordeal is not over until you're out of the building and away from the premises. Even the friendly chap you bump into in the queue at the coffee shop round the corner where you go to recover might actually be one of the recruiting team.

Finally, you have to accept that not every interview will lead to an offer. If you get a rejection letter, write or email back and thank them for their time and encouragement. Ask specifically for feedback that might help you next time. This feedback sometimes is painful to listen to, but listen all the same. You need all the help you can get so don't leave any opportunity untouched.

Action plan: coping with redundancy

Redundancy can feel like a kick in the teeth. In reality it is often a boot up the backside, giving you the incentive to take a fresh look at the work you do. Within a year of redundancy, most people over 50 are settled into something new. It might not be what they first expected to do, but they are invariably happy. Here's what to do if you're worried about redundancy:

- **If you think there's a risk, prepare a plan B.** Work on the sections of this chapter that will help you be ready should it happen. Be prepared but don't worry about it unduly unless it happens.
- **Keep calm.** If it happens to you, stay calm and don't panic. Work though this chapter; seek advice from specialists and, if you're lucky, an outplacement consultant hired by your employer. Do nothing quickly; take your time.
- **Stay positive.** It's a tough time, but letting it get you down will make it tougher. Make time in your job-hunting life to work on your fitness and your relationship. Don't work yourself into the ground. Stay positive.
- **Celebrate successes.** Even if you don't get the job, being interviewed can be a huge achievement. Remember that at interviews it's as much about personal chemistry as skills and experience. Celebrate your successes.

One final thought on the subject of redundancy. It may never happen to you, but the tips in this chapter can help you be an understanding friend or perhaps even a compassionate boss. We can all help soften the blow of redundancy if we try.

12

work–life balance

In this chapter you will learn:
- how to develop a career portfolio
- how to widen your horizons
- how to set goals for the future.

Three generations ago, men would work until they were 65, then retire and soon afterwards die. Life expectancy in the early twentieth century was surprisingly lower than it is today. Even your father probably worked up to retirement age and then abruptly stopped.

You, however, have far more choice than any of the generations that went before. We are told that everyone will need to work beyond the normal retirement age. That actually will prove to be beneficial to many of us. This chapter will help you make sure that you benefit from a staged retirement, rather than an endless slog followed by years of inactivity.

Re-defining retirement

To consider retirement objectively you may need to change the way you view it. Full retirement is that time when you live entirely on your investments and savings. The most significant part of these investments is usually your pension.

However, pensions are now much more flexible than they ever have been before. You can delay taking your pension and let the money continue to grow. You can also take your pension in stages and, if you decide never to stop work, you can pass your pension fund on to your heirs, although it will probably be treated as part of your estate and taxed.

In terms of activity, the notion of retirement becomes more interesting. Ask people what they want to do in retirement and they'll say things like:

'I want to do as I please and not have to get up and go to work.'

'I want time to pursue my hobbies and interests and travel with my partner.'

'I want to stay healthy and enjoy seeing my grandchildren grow up.'

If you think about it, you don't need to be fully retired to do any of these things. You simply need more time off and a greater sense of control over your life. What you might actually need is to adjust your work–life balance to give you more flexibility.

Developing a portfolio career

It was the management guru Charles Handy who first coined the phrase 'portfolio career'. He used it to describe where people had no full-time job, but instead had a number of part-time, or peripatetic roles.

You on the other hand are probably in full-time work and wondering how to find more time for you in a hectic schedule. The portfolio approach might hold the answer for you.

As you can see, developing a portfolio of activities means you can enjoy a greater degree of freedom now. Then, when you want to retire, you simply let some of the activities go. Although you might find that the portfolio will simply evolve with different things filling your time as you grow closer to old age.

Here are some tips to help you transform your current work into a more flexible portfolio:

Negotiate the option

If you currently work full time, you need to look at the option of making that more flexible. You might start by trading a cut in pay for longer holidays, or better perhaps, a four-day week. That gives you a day for something else.

Job sharing is becoming more popular these days. Whilst for some jobs it is difficult to share, others actually benefit from being shared. There is truth in the old adage that, 'two heads are better than one'. The first move though, is usually made by the incumbent employee. Here's how to do it:

- work out how your job could be shared and what time split suits you
- discuss the idea with your manager; show them the company benefits
- your contract of employment is changed and a job sharer recruited
- you and your job sharer both become permanent part-timers.

In some cases, the person seeking a job share actually knows who they'd like to share with. Clearly the employer needs to be comfortable with this, but it can make life easier if you share with someone you know. Clearly you don't want to job share with your partner. You'd have little time together!

Identify the gaps

Having worked out how to make more time, you now need to decide what you are going to do with it. If you don't need the income, you might simply develop a hobby or do voluntary work. More likely though is that you will want to still earn money, but in a completely different way.

Here are some ideas you might consider:

Work for yourself
If you have always wanted to work for yourself, why not do so part time. Providing you're not competing with your employer, this should not be a problem. Perhaps you love music and would like to teach youngsters how to play an instrument, or enjoy gardening and would like to tidy other people's gardens for money.

Another part-time job
You probably don't want two very similar part-time jobs, but two that are different might be fine. If the two jobs contrast quite markedly, you will find the difference and the variety stimulating. Inspiration for one will strike when you're doing the other. You rarely become stale with a portfolio career!

Travel
Could an undergraduate keep your job ticking over for the summer months? If so, why not work for nine months and travel for three?

Non-exec director
Many public bodies have non-executive boards. These are made up of people with a range of skills, which are not always related to the activity of the organization. Vacancies are always advertised. Most pay their non-execs who work for around 25 days a year.

Making it happen

Human nature is such that you will find plenty of excuses to put off doing anything as radical as developing a portfolio career. The obstacles might seem large but are in reality rarely insurmountable.

A fringe benefit of the portfolio career is that you have more control over your working life. You no longer rely on one employer for all of your income. Now there are two or more. You are in control!

Stuart

After 20 years in the planning department of his local authority, Stuart was beginning to feel stir-crazy. He was almost beginning to count the days until he could retire and draw his pension. Promotion would mean moving to a new city and he didn't want to do that. He knew he had more to give, yet was stuck in the very familiar routine of a job he no longer found exciting.

He decided he'd like to try job sharing and with the time this freed up, joined a training company as an associate. Now he works three days a week at City Hall and each week, travels somewhere different to run workshops for newly-qualified planners. Life has suddenly become far more enjoyable.

Phasing your retirement

When you finally decide you want to retire (and that's probably many years away) it doesn't have to be abrupt change. All that applies in the previous section to job sharing and portfolio working also applies to retirement.

The difference is that instead of creating a portfolio of jobs, you broaden that out to create a portfolio of activities. Those activities might include playing golf every Wednesday, to break up the working week. What you want to achieve is a gradual switch from employed work to things you enjoy, but that do not necessarily pay.

In many ways, the men who seem to enjoy retirement most, are those who keep themselves busy. They schedule their days and weeks as if they were still working. They get lots done, have lots of fun and live long.

Contrast this with the chap who stops work, then sits at home wondering how to fill his time. Life soon gets boring and that's when the problems start.

You're too far from retiring now to devote a lot of time to planning how you'll spend it. However, if your employer is looking at the long-term structure of the organization, knowing you'd prefer to phase your retirement over a number of years will help them. As well as giving you more flexibility, it does the same for your employer.

William

After spending his entire career in the building trade, William worked through his 50s as yard foreman at a builder's merchant. His knowledge was invaluable, particularly to the many do-it-yourself customers who visited on Saturday mornings.

Being part of a large group, they had a strict retirement policy and William was unable to negotiate a phased retirement. However, his branch manager knew how people bought more when reassured by William that they could tackle the job. He hired William after he retired to spend every Friday and Saturday advising customers. This 'new service' was advertised and proved a great success. William's fee for his time came from the branch manager's marketing budget. Everybody gained and no company rules were broken.

Discovering new interests

It could be that you are a confirmed workaholic with few other interests. The idea of a job portfolio has little appeal, yet you know you need to broaden your horizons. Taking evening classes or going birdwatching are certainly not on your agenda. You want to achieve things, not simply pass the time.

We all need to constantly search out new interests and activities. Things change, as do our circumstances and the more you are stimulated by the new, the more you will enjoy life.

Here are some simple ways you might broaden your horizons and discover possible new interests:

Retreat

It might sound strange to discover how to do more by doing less. However, the process of isolating yourself from all that currently occupies your mind lets new ideas flood in. You might take part in an organized retreat, where you are part of a group, with an expert facilitator. Alternatively, you might organize your own retreat. Here's how to do it:

Where

You simply need to get away from all distraction for at least one day and ideally three or four. There are directories of places you can go and stay, where you may eat, sleep and be left alone to think. There is often someone there you can talk to at various times during your retreat if you find that would be helpful. Alternatively, you might simply pack a rucksack and walk to the top of a hill where you can comfortably spend a day alone with your thoughts.

When

There is no simple answer to when. The first time you go on retreat it will feel very strange and you will find it difficult making the time to do it. However, when you've been once, even if only for a day, it's good to repeat the exercise annually.

How

It's good to make notes on retreat. You can review and update them on subsequent retreats. This shows you the progress your life is making. Some people buy a bound book of lined paper and use this to make and review retreat notes for many years.

Who

Sometimes it's good to go on retreat with your partner, particularly if your relationship is long established. Things you might want to change will inevitably impact on your partner and vice versa. Most commonly though, people retreat on their own.

Meet different people

It's surprising how few people we actually get to know well over a lifetime. We are surrounded by people for most of the time, but most simply form part of the crowd.

If you look at the places you go and the groups you mix with, you will realize that there are huge swathes of the local population you don't know and may not even fully understand.

If you want to broaden your mind, it's good to meet people you would normally never encounter. Their views, attitudes and experiences will challenge your own perceptions and introduce you to new ideas. For example, you might consider:

- becoming a prison visitor and talking to offenders
- organizing an exchange visit where you swap jobs for a month with someone in another country

- travelling off the tourist trails, meeting and talking with people from different cultures
- changing your habits – commute by bus for a week rather than car and talk to your fellow passengers.

Start learning

Of course you've probably attended many training courses through your work, but what about learning new things? It's not just about attending evening classes, but more about opening your mind. We all get stuck in our ways and it's good to break down some of those barriers.

Here are some ways to learn that you might not have considered:

Read wider

Reading books is a great way to broaden your mind. If you've not read much recently, try buying or borrowing some books and giving it a try. Try both fiction and non fiction. Consider joining a book club where you read then discuss one book each month.

Make music

We often learn an instrument as a boy, then give up before really becoming proficient. Why not become a musician? If you become good enough, you could join an amateur orchestra or band. It's also a good way to meet new and interesting people.

Return to university

You don't need to become a full-time student. Universities today offer a wide range of part-time courses that combined, can give you a degree. If you are in business, why not consider a part-time MBA? It will energize you at work!

It's never too late to take up a new interest. People discover new hobbies or learn new skills in their 80s and 90s. You're a lot younger than that. Stimulate your mind and see what develops; surprise yourself!

Making space

One of the problems with modern life is that we all try to do too much. Every waking moment is taken up with some activity or other. We even do two or more things at once (for example, drive, listen to the radio and use our hands-free mobile phone).

Being constantly busy means that you actually stop noticing what's going on around you. Days turn into weeks into years. Time flies and you don't notice it happening. If you've read to this point and thought, 'yes I'd like to do these things, but haven't the time', you need to de-clutter your life. It's not time management, more a way to ditch the things you no longer need to do. Here are some ideas to help you do that:

Clear your mind

Try writing things down rather than trying to remember everything. It sounds almost too simple, but it works. Use a paper or PC-based diary and jot down when you have to do things. Then forget about them until the time comes.

Your mind can also become cluttered with 'baggage'. That's the stuff that eats you up inside when you can't let go of a mistake or insoluble problem. Try to put the past to one side and let the things you can't change go. Clear your mind and there'll be space for new, more positive things.

Clear your emotions

Feelings, particularly our feelings about other people, can give us more anxiety than those deadlines or domestic dramas. Past relationships, together with past experiences can really mess up your emotions, even decades later.

Sometimes, a few sessions with a counsellor or psychotherapist can help you clear out your emotional baggage. As you seek balance in your life, removing deeply-rooted emotional baggage can liberate your capacity to love life more.

Clear your body

There's been a lot written about the way our bodies take in and retain various toxins. There are also many theories about how you can detox your body. Some have validity, whilst other are perhaps more doubtful.

What is certain is that most of us would benefit from ridding our bodies of excess weight. Developing a trim, fit body is a good way to make it more efficient. You can get more done if you feel physically good.

Clear your address book

Over the years we all collect people. Most of us have former school chums with whom we exchange Christmas cards and not much else. Then there are the people you have outgrown; the ones you seem to have less in common with every time you meet.

You can drop people tactfully and painlessly, by simply taking them out of your address book. You stop being the one who takes the initiative and don't contact them any more. If your relationship means something to them, they'll be in touch. If it doesn't, they won't. Perhaps they'll be as relieved as you are to focus harder on the people who mean more to them.

Clear your home

Have a major clear-out of all the stuff you no longer need. Work through your home and also perhaps your place of work. Don't forget your garage and your car. If you've not used something for a while, chuck it, sell it or give it away.

Action plan: how to actually change your work–life balance

This chapter describes many facets of the work–life balance. You will have come to appreciate as you read through, that there are things you can change. In fact, for most of us the greatest opportunity is to feel that we're in control. The feeling that others are controlling too much of our lives is one of the greatest causes of depression and anxiety. We should all be striving to live our own lives, not let others impose their agendas upon us.

Over the next 20 years you will probably want to make the transition from working full time to playing full time. The time to start making changes though is now. Regaining control of your life will empower you more than you might imagine. So how do you shift the inertia and actually make a start? Here is a five-point checklist to get you started:

1 **Make a 20-year chart.** This must be kept really simple, but make a table with 20 boxes, labelling them as the years they represent. You need a long column of boxes, starting today and ending in 20 years' time.

2 **Fill in the boxes.** Write in the top of each box the key factors that for you will make each year well balanced in terms of how you spend your time. Underneath each of these headings, add the single biggest obstacle to that vision being realized.

3 **Create an action plan.** This is where you focus on the things you need to do now, in order to make the thing you've planned for the future happen. For example:

- A world cruise in five years' time might need you to both increase your savings and arrange sabbatical leave from work when the time comes.

- Being a fantastic granddad in two years' time might mean changing your working day to enable you to collect your grandchild from school when he or she starts.

4 **Share your plan.** You need to make yourself accountable and that means giving someone close to you the right to ask for regular progress reports. It's easier to make changes when you know you'll be asked about them and chastised if you've slipped behind.

5 **Do it.** There will always be reasons to postpone making changes. Your own feelings of guilt at doing things that are just for you will also tend to hold you back. When it comes down to it, you simply need to be a little bit self-centred and just do it. No one else will change your life for you!

13

volunteering

In this chapter you will learn:
- why putting something back is good for you too
- how to find the right volunteering opportunity
- how to campaign for change.

It is too easy to dismiss volunteering as something that do-gooders indulge in that has little relevance to us. In fact, volunteering in its broadest sense is a fascinating world, filled with opportunities. When tackled properly, volunteering represents a fair exchange between the volunteer and the cause. The value you gain from any volunteering activity should be at least equal to the effort you put in. Volunteering is for you as well as those your efforts help.

Naturally the high streets remain full of sweet old ladies shaking collecting tins. You could argue that this activity gives them a good reason to get up, dress smartly and venture into town. They may also be lonely and so relish the chance of conversation with strangers. The money they collect, albeit in modest amounts, helps further a cause they care about.

However, you perhaps want to use volunteering to make some changes to your life; to broaden your perspective and much more. Successful volunteering is about finding a win:win, not self-sacrifice or pure altruism.

Why volunteering is important for everyone

There is little doubt that volunteering helps make things happen. Even in the most generous society, government funding is never enough to meet every need. Just as you are probably very able to cope with life and all it throws at you, others are not. We all face challenges, but some need the help and support of others to overcome the things that hold them back.

And it's not just about people. With more than six billion people living on this planet, just about every aspect of our environment, both natural and man-made also needs help. You are never short of things to do.

There is also a blurred boundary between self-interest and the common good. For example, if your street is always untidy, you have more to gain than anyone else from making it tidy again. Furthermore, if everyone clubbed together to hire a skip, then spent a Saturday morning spring-cleaning the street, it would create a real sense of community and purpose amongst all who lived there.

Volunteering has another important role, particularly for men in their 50s. It can help them to feel needed, at a time of life when sometimes people feel you are a little past it. In fact, many people find the transition from work to retirement eased considerably by their overlapping involvement in various voluntary organizations.

Why volunteering is important for you

Whatever work you do, you almost inevitably only see a thin slice of life in your neighbourhood, industry sector or country. As you come to explore outside your immediate surroundings, you discover that actually, everything is interdependent. Gaining an understanding of the wider world helps you achieve more where you are.

Specific benefits of volunteering include:

Confidence building

Being a volunteer creates opportunities for you to do things you would normally not do. For example, if you do not manage people, but find yourself running a club, you gain experience of managing and motivating others. The great thing about that scenario is that once you join any club, it's actually difficult not to end up with some responsibility.

This kind of experience can also enhance your CV and provide a valuable discussion point at interviews. In fact, if you've been made redundant after a lengthy time with one employer, but have been involved in lots of out-of-work activities, that broader experience will make it easier for recruiters to select you for interview. It shows you're someone who does things, rather than simply wait for things to happen to you.

Free training

In many respects, volunteering can teach you many new skills. Activities that involve supervising, influencing or motivating people can all provide valuable management experience. That's useful if you're studying for a qualification and need to demonstrate that you have actually carried out a wider range of business processes than your current job allows.

Equally important is the opportunity for you to provide free training. Teaching others a skill they need, that you have, is a great way of reinforcing and developing that skill in yourself.

For example, if your day job involves advising companies on complex HR issues, helping a small charity hire its first salaried worker will take you right back to basics. It's surprising how over the years you forget just how naïve people can be when they first encounter a new situation.

A wider network

You can't know enough people. That's not to say you need to widen your social circle or work at keeping in touch with everyone you meet. Your wider network should contain everyone you've met that you feel might one day be useful to you. Keeping their details handy is often all you need to do.

If you get to know new people through voluntary work, you meet people you would not get to know through your normal day-to-day life. Clearly you should not seek to exploit those contacts. It's more a case of having within your network people who know you, that you can trust, who are able to help you solve a problem.

Put something back

The voluntary sector is full of people putting something back. Often they have benefited in some kind from the activity of the group or organization they now help. Going back as a volunteer gives them tremendous empathy with the cause. It also helps them to stay on track.

Brian

A talented artist and gallery owner, due to a variety of work and personal pressures, Brian became an alcoholic. He was eventually persuaded to join his local Alcoholics Anonymous group and with their help, was able to give up the booze.

Part of the philosophy of that organization is that the risk of returning to excessive drinking is always present. Additionally, people in the depths of their crisis take considerable encouragement from meeting people who have overcome the seemingly insurmountable barrier they are themselves struggling with.

For Brian, this means he was encouraged to remain with the group long after he needed its help. He spends time every week helping other people recover from the addiction that so disrupted his life.

How to find suitable volunteering opportunities

As you might expect, there are a number of matchmaking agencies, themselves charities, which introduce potential volunteers to volunteering opportunities. They tend to have different names in different places so the best way to find one is to search the internet, or ask at the local Chamber of Commerce.

Naturally if you want to include volunteering within your portfolio of activities, you want to choose something about which you can become enthusiastic, if not passionate. Here to stimulate your imagination are some areas you might or might not have thought about:

Health

The health sector contains many voluntary organizations. Some focus their attention on a particular medical condition, whilst others focus on improving healthcare for potentially excluded community groups.

Many of the services delivered in the field of mental health are provided by voluntary organizations. These can range from a small counselling service to a massive national charity that contracts with the government and provides services on its behalf.

A key need with many healthcare organizations is to stay in touch with the communities they serve. Many of the larger organizations have consultative groups drawn from the community. Membership of these groups can be as fascinating and valuable as being more hands on.

Education

This sector is similar in many respects to health. Many organizations exist to help those who find learning difficult to enjoy a good level of education and training. Organizations that work with children cover the full spectrum from the very able, who need additional stimulation, to the severely disadvantaged who also benefit hugely from more individual support.

Often overlooked is the fact that state-run schools rely heavily on volunteers. From helping in the classroom, to fundraising to buy a minibus, the opportunities are endless. There are also initiatives that link employers with schools, so this aspect of volunteering can take place at work.

Environment

Many people feel passionately about the environment. Some choose to campaign for policy change, whilst others are content to spend a weekend clearing scrubland. May carry out wildlife surveys or take part in activities designed to raise public awareness of the issues.

If you spend your week tied to a desk in an air conditioned office, you might welcome the opportunity to spend some of your spare time doing physical work outside.

Government

As well as becoming a local politician, which is itself a form of volunteering, government offers additional opportunities. Many campaigns and projects are created by the public sector as a result of research or consultation.

To succeed, however, these initiatives need the energy and commitment of people willing to give their time to actually make things happen. Providing money and a strategy is rarely enough. It takes people on the ground to produce real results.

Overseas

Many aid agencies are recognizing that people of all ages want to work overseas. You might consider a post-retirement gap-year, or just take a three-month sabbatical from work to travel.

To find an overseas volunteering opportunity, talk to large aid organizations, specialist agencies such as VSO or watch for advertised opportunities.

As you are beginning to see, there are a multitude of different volunteering opportunities. Some are obvious, others less so. Some people look for an existing need, whilst others find a need and create a solution. As you move through your 50s, you will almost inevitably want to get involved with new things. Volunteering can make that possible.

How to become a neighbourhood activist

Neighbourhood activism should be close to everyone's heart. We all want to live in a 'good neighbourhood'. It's a place where things seem to happen, the shops don't close and get boarded up and where crime levels are low.

They are also places people want to live. This means house prices rise, which makes investing in your community financially smart as well. It can make good sense to become a neighbourhood activist.

Every neighbourhood has the potential to become a better and safer place to live and work. Key to improving any area is to encourage those who live there to develop a sense of ownership of the place. Your opportunity is to be the catalyst that sparks the local revolution.

What makes a good neighbourhood?

Here are some factors that people say make a place nicer to live:

- **Public space.** Parks, gardens, squares and footpaths, all encourage people out of their homes where they can meet each other.
- **Privacy.** You also need to be alone at times and no one likes to feel their home is overlooked.
- **Transport not traffic.** Easy access to shops, work and leisure gives people time. Traffic, however, pollutes so a compromise is necessary.
- **Friends.** Older people grew up in a time when everyone knew everyone. People didn't move about so much and lived their lives close to each other. This intimacy creates a feeling of belonging.
- **Few commuters.** If your estate empties every morning, leaving just the elderly and those caring for children, it can seem barren. You want people living and working locally. This creates energy and buzz.

Making it happen

You don't need to do much to become a neighbourhood activist, just a little more than you're doing right now. Most people are content to wait for others to take the lead. You are different to other people; you are going to make the first moves. Here are some simple ideas to get you started:

- **Listen to gripes.** You need to be sure you're not the only one who sees the challenge. Ask around and see if what's bugging you is also bugging others.

- **Pick up litter.** If others see you picking up litter they'll take the hint and do the same. More importantly, the people who drop it will be less inclined to do so. It's harder to drop litter in a clean street.
- **Report damage.** Streetlights not working? Road signs bent? Potholes full of water? You can be the person who reports it; others will just moan.
- **Scrounge the paint.** Bus shelters and other communal facilities quickly get tatty. Scrounge some paint and brushes. Start painting!
- **Organize a gardening competition.** Find a sponsor to provide judges and a prize. Your whole street will suddenly become much neater!
- **Celebrate national holidays.** Street parties are great fun. Everyone helps prepare, but it needs you to suggest the idea and get things moving.
- **Visit the seaside.** If you live in a large city, organize a collection and hire a coach. Take everyone to the seaside for the day. If some families cannot afford to pay, let them come anyway. Include everyone.
- **Organize petitions.** If you don't want a supermarket built right behind your street, get everyone to sign a petition. It's the best way to muster a large number of objectors.
- **Lead the bid.** Very often, councils and local trusts offer grants to small community projects. Coordinate the bid and your playing field or community centre could benefit. Only those who bid get money!
- **Run for council.** Be a candidate for your local council elections. Stand as an Independent and let people vote for you, not a political party.

How to be a successful campaigner

Campaigns are usually started because you and others feel very strongly about a particular topic. You want to change the way something is done, or perhaps force others' hands so that the issue you're passionate about is dealt with properly. Campaigns are often fuelled by emotion.

To succeed, you need to remain objective. Here are some things to do:

- **Be objective.** Campaigners who lose their tempers rarely win. If they really go over the top, they can sometimes even end up in jail.

- **Know your goals.** You must identify exactly what you want to make happen. Simply wanting to make things 'better' will not do. Goals have to be measurable.
- **Be realistic.** The best campaigns are those that have simple objectives. Once these are achieved, you can set further, tougher objectives.
- **Celebrate.** Victories can be hard won. Don't push your successes to one side to continue the fight. Take time to celebrate success.
- **Be polite.** You may be confronted by people with diametrically opposite views to your own. Everyone is entitled to their own views. Change minds by debate, not by shouting down your opposition.
- **Build a team.** The more people who declare their support for your campaign, the more likely you are to succeed. Even petitions help this.
- **Spread the word.** You need to generate press coverage. That is one of the best ways to gain support and influence public opinion.
- **Lobby people with power.** You need the support of people with the right connections. They can put in a good word for you and endorse your campaign. Internet research can often unearth a celebrity who might feel the same was as you.
- **Persist.** If you give up too easily, you will never succeed. You need to keep banging the drum so that people tire of hearing it.
- **Adapt.** Sometimes the ground moves and things change. Be alert to the risk and be ready to adapt. Do not become out of touch.

Generating publicity for your campaigns

If you are leading a campaign, or are perhaps just one of a group seeking to bring about some kind of change, publicity is vital if you are to have an impact. Here are some ways you can generate free publicity:

Visualize your campaign

If you want to raise £100,000, (or indeed $100 000 or 1000 000 Euro) what does this amount look like? How tall is a pile of pound coins/dollars/euros? Create some striking images in the minds of the people you want to influence.

Quantify your need

If you need 100 volunteers, say so. If to raise your target amount you need 20,000 donors, count them as they give. How many bus loads do you need?

Get credible support

Campaigns to change the way illnesses are treated need endorsement by medical specialists. You need expert support to be taken seriously.

Arrange stunts

Good publicity stunts:

- are photogenic and professionally photographed
- are safe and do not put people or property at risk
- coincide with and perhaps hijack an existing event.

Issue news releases

Good news releases follow this formula:

- a strong, memorable, relevant headline
- a picture that illustrates the headline
- one paragraph containing the key points you're making
- a second paragraph explaining why it's important
- a third stating clearly what you want readers to do
- contact details so that journalists can call you – remember this might well be in the evening or at the weekend.

They are also emailed straight to the journalists most likely to cover the story (so research is vital) and are always followed up by phone.

Taking public office

Some volunteering opportunities can raise your profile more than others. Taking public office is one way you can volunteer in a way that puts you in the public eye. This is good if you enjoy publicity; less so if you prefer to steer clear of controversy.

Public office can help you make that transition from critic to activist. It's so easy to knock those who put themselves forward to take office; when you join their ranks, you discover that it's never as straightforward as you thought.

Examples of roles you might consider include standing for election to your local council, becoming a magistrate or joining the board of a quango.

Action plan: making it happen

Volunteering can do so much for you: broaden your mind, develop your abilities, expand your network and most importantly of all, make a real difference to a cause you care about. Once you put your head above the parapet and get involved in one area, you will find that other opportunities present themselves to you.

You need to be able to tactfully say 'no', as well as to say 'yes' if you are not to be overwhelmed. Being enthusiastic and overcommitted is dangerous. It makes you feel overwhelmed and unable to cope. Those you are helping feel let down because you're not delivering all that they hoped and perhaps you promised.

It is particularly difficult to manage the extent of your involvement when it's a cause close to your heart. You can see and even feel the need. There are always more tasks than hours and it's all too easy to say yes, then struggle to find the time.

Here then is a final checklist to help you find the right opportunity, then avoid saying yes to too much!

- **What do you care about?** You need to start with the cause. What is it you really care about? What personal experiences have you had that would help others? Equally, what are you not at all interested in?
- **What can you trade?** Be objective and work out what skills you have that will benefit a voluntary organization. Equally, decide what you want in return. Do you need to develop new skills, or simply meet new people? Perhaps you just want to feel you're doing something useful.
- **Who can you help?** It should not be too difficult to find a cause to support. It might be a local group, or a national organization with a very specific focus. Check them out and ask for information.
- **Don't offer too much.** Take your relationship one step at a time. Don't offer to do too much at first. Also, set some ground rules and suggest a probationary period. You want to be able to leave without bad feeling if it doesn't work out as you'd hoped.

- **Think before you speak.** In meetings there is always talk about new opportunities. Don't jump in straight away and volunteer. Take your time to think through how much time you actually have to spare. Don't get in deeper than you can realistically manage.

- **Review regularly.** There comes a time, and it can be quite soon, when you've given all you can and moving on to a new campaign is wise. Many organizations do not let trustees serve for more than six years, although in many cases that is actually too long! Don't stay longer than you feel you need to. There are always others coming along behind waiting to be persuaded to fill your shoes!

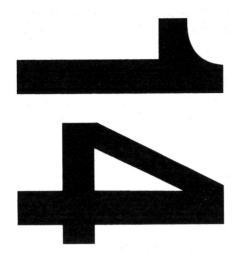

14

final thoughts

Whatever people may tell you, or more importantly, you might tell yourself, 50 is a turning point in your life. You are exactly halfway to your century and so it's possible you have as long to live as you have lived so far. Cast your mind back to your earliest memory. Perhaps you were two or three. It was an awfully long time ago. Then you had few skills, little knowledge and even crossing the street unaided would have been risky.

Today you have vast reservoir of knowledge, experience and skill. You've seen some good times and learned some tough lessons along the way. The clock cannot be turned back, it can only tick forward.

You now face the second half of your life. Unlike when you were a baby, you have the benefit of 50 years' life experience behind you. How are you going to use that experience? What are you going to achieve? Who are you going to spend these next few decades with? The choices are boundless.

At 50 your father probably wore a cardigan, smoked a pipe and decided that he was now on the downward slope so he might as well sit back and let it happen. Mine certainly did that. Five years later he was dead; killed by inactivity, alcohol and tobacco. I don't plan to let that happen to me and nor should you.

Whatever your life looks like today, you have within you the potential to make tomorrow better. You can never regain your youth, but with the wisdom that only comes with age and maturity, you don't need that physical strength to bring about the changes in your life that deep down you want to see.

Now turn back through the book again. Mark the passages that resonate most loudly with you. Highlight the actions you plan to take, grasp your 50s with both hands and make this decade one you will always look back on as your best. Good luck!

taking it further

The best way to find out more about any topic mentioned in this book is to search the internet. That way you will find out the very latest information about the areas you want to explore further.

There are a number of useful websites where you might start. These include:

Age Concern, works with all over 50s: **www.ageconcern.co.uk**
Age Positive, a UK government initiative: **www.agepositive. gov.uk**
University of the Third Age, learning for the over 50s: **www.u3a.org.uk**
Credit Action, independent debt advice: **www.creditaction.org.uk**
The UK Government Pensions Service: **www.thepensionservice.gov.uk**
Third Age Employment Network, advice on getting a job: **www.taen.org.uk**
Prime, supporting over 50s into self-employment: **www.primeinitiative.org.uk**
NHS Direct, online and telephone health advice: **www.nhsdirect.nhs.uk**

Here are some more useful websites that might help you dig deeper into some of the topics covered in this book.

Adults shops – **http://www.annsummers.com**
Become a magistrate – **http://www.magistrates-association.org.uk**
Chambers of Commerce – **http://www.chamberonline.co.uk**
Community organisations – **http://www.ncvo-vol.org.uk/**
Debt advice – **http://www.nationaldebtline.co.uk/**
Education/businesslinks – **http://www.nebpn.org**

Environmental work – http://www.wildlifetrusts.org/
IFAs – http://www.unbiased.co.uk
Jobs – http://www.monster.co.uk
Overseas volunteering – http://www.vso.org.uk/
Prince's Trust – http://www.princes-trust.org.uk/
Psychotherapy – http://www.baco.co.uk
Redundancy – http://www.ran-advice.co.uk
Relationships – http://www.relate.org.uk/
Retreats – http://www.thegoodretreatguide.com/
Run a marathon – http://www.runnersworld.co.uk
Stop smoking – http://www.givingupsmoking.co.uk/
Volunteering – http://www.volunteering.org.uk/
Work discrimination – http://www.adviceguide.org.uk/

index

teach® yourself

From Advanced Sudoku to Zulu, you'll find everything you need in the **teach yourself** range, in books, on CD and on DVD.

Visit **www.teachyourself.co.uk** for more details.

Advanced Sudoku and Kakuro
Afrikaans
Alexander Technique
Algebra
Ancient Greek
Applied Psychology
Arabic
Aromatherapy
Art History
Astrology
Astronomy
AutoCAD 2004
AutoCAD 2007
Ayurveda
Baby Massage and Yoga
Baby Signing
Baby Sleep
Bach Flower Remedies
Backgammon
Ballroom Dancing
Basic Accounting
Basic Computer Skills
Basic Mathematics
Beauty
Beekeeping
Beginner's Arabic Script
Beginner's Chinese Script
Beginner's Dutch

Beginner's French
Beginner's German
Beginner's Greek
Beginner's Greek Script
Beginner's Hindi
Beginner's Italian
Beginner's Japanese
Beginner's Japanese Script
Beginner's Latin
Beginner's Mandarin Chinese
Beginner's Portuguese
Beginner's Russian
Beginner's Russian Script
Beginner's Spanish
Beginner's Turkish
Beginner's Urdu Script
Bengali
Better Bridge
Better Chess
Better Driving
Better Handwriting
Biblical Hebrew
Biology
Birdwatching
Blogging
Body Language
Book Keeping
Brazilian Portuguese

Bridge
British Empire, The
British Monarchy from Henry VIII, The
Buddhism
Bulgarian
Business Chinese
Business French
Business Japanese
Business Plans
Business Spanish
Business Studies
Buying a Home in France
Buying a Home in Italy
Buying a Home in Portugal
Buying a Home in Spain
C++
Calculus
Calligraphy
Cantonese
Car Buying and Maintenance
Card Games
Catalan
Chess
Chi Kung
Chinese Medicine
Christianity
Classical Music
Coaching
Cold War, The
Collecting
Computing for the Over 50s
Consulting
Copywriting
Correct English
Counselling
Creative Writing
Cricket
Croatian
Crystal Healing
CVs
Czech
Danish
Decluttering
Desktop Publishing
Detox

Digital Home Movie Making
Digital Photography
Dog Training
Drawing
Dream Interpretation
Dutch
Dutch Conversation
Dutch Dictionary
Dutch Grammar
Eastern Philosophy
Electronics
English as a Foreign Language
English for International Business
English Grammar
English Grammar as a Foreign Language
English Vocabulary
Entrepreneurship
Estonian
Ethics
Excel 2003
Feng Shui
Film Making
Film Studies
Finance for Non-Financial Managers
Finnish
First World War, The
Fitness
Flash 8
Flash MX
Flexible Working
Flirting
Flower Arranging
Franchising
French
French Conversation
French Dictionary
French Grammar
French Phrasebook
French Starter Kit
French Verbs
French Vocabulary
Freud
Gaelic

Gardening
Genetics
Geology
German
German Conversation
German Grammar
German Phrasebook
German Verbs
German Vocabulary
Globalization
Go
Golf
Good Study Skills
Great Sex
Greek
Greek Conversation
Greek Phrasebook
Growing Your Business
Guitar
Gulf Arabic
Hand Reflexology
Hausa
Herbal Medicine
Hieroglyphics
Hindi
Hindi Conversation
Hinduism
History of Ireland, The
Home PC Maintenance and
  Networking
How to DJ
How to Run a Marathon
How to Win at Casino Games
How to Win at Horse Racing
How to Win at Online Gambling
How to Win at Poker
How to Write a Blockbuster
Human Anatomy & Physiology
Hungarian
Icelandic
Improve Your French
Improve Your German
Improve Your Italian
Improve Your Spanish
Improving Your Employability

Indian Head Massage
Indonesian
Instant French
Instant German
Instant Greek
Instant Italian
Instant Japanese
Instant Portuguese
Instant Russian
Instant Spanish
Internet, The
Irish
Irish Conversation
Irish Grammar
Islam
Italian
Italian Conversation
Italian Grammar
Italian Phrasebook
Italian Starter Kit
Italian Verbs
Italian Vocabulary
Japanese
Japanese Conversation
Java
JavaScript
Jazz
Jewellery Making
Judaism
Jung
Kama Sutra, The
Keeping Aquarium Fish
Keeping Pigs
Keeping Poultry
Keeping a Rabbit
Knitting
Korean
Latin
Latin American Spanish
Latin Dictionary
Latin Grammar
Latvian
Letter Writing Skills
Life at 50: For Men
Life at 50: For Women

Life Coaching
Linguistics
LINUX
Lithuanian
Magic
Mahjong
Malay
Managing Stress
Managing Your Own Career
Mandarin Chinese
Mandarin Chinese Conversation
Marketing
Marx
Massage
Mathematics
Meditation
Middle East Since 1945, The
Modern China
Modern Hebrew
Modern Persian
Mosaics
Music Theory
Mussolini's Italy
Nazi Germany
Negotiating
Nepali
New Testament Greek
NLP
Norwegian
Norwegian Conversation
Old English
One-Day French
One-Day French – the DVD
One-Day German
One-Day Greek
One-Day Italian
One-Day Portuguese
One-Day Spanish
One-Day Spanish – the DVD
Origami
Owning a Cat
Owning a Horse
Panjabi
PC Networking for Small
  Businesses

Personal Safety and Self
  Defence
Philosophy
Philosophy of Mind
Philosophy of Religion
Photography
Photoshop
PHP with MySQL
Physics
Piano
Pilates
Planning Your Wedding
Polish
Polish Conversation
Politics
Portuguese
Portuguese Conversation
Portuguese Grammar
Portuguese Phrasebook
Postmodernism
Pottery
PowerPoint 2003
PR
Project Management
Psychology
Quick Fix French Grammar
Quick Fix German Grammar
Quick Fix Italian Grammar
Quick Fix Spanish Grammar
Quick Fix: Access 2002
Quick Fix: Excel 2000
Quick Fix: Excel 2002
Quick Fix: HTML
Quick Fix: Windows XP
Quick Fix: Word
Quilting
Recruitment
Reflexology
Reiki
Relaxation
Retaining Staff
Romanian
Running Your Own Business
Russian
Russian Conversation